One Man's Family

ONE MAN'S FAMILY

A Single Father and His Children

LINLEY M. STAFFORD

Random House   New York

Copyright © 1978 by Linley M. Stafford
All rights reserved under International and Pan-American Copyright Conventions.
Published in the United States by Random House, Inc., New York, and simultaneously in Canada by Random House of Canada Limited, Toronto.

Library of Congress Cataloging in Publication Data
Stafford, Linley M
One man's family.
1. Stafford, Linley M. 2. Fathers—United States—Biography. 3. Single-parent family—United States. 4. Father and child. I. Title.
HQ756.S73 301.42'7 78-57125
ISBN 0-394-42465-4

Manufactured in the United States of America
2 4 6 8 9 7 5 3
First Edition

To Preston and Molly
 who helped me understand what being a parent really means . . .

One Man's Family

I

My eleven-year-old son was sobbing uncontrollably in my arms. "But why can't I live with you? You are my father. I love you and want to live with you."

"I very much want you to live with me, Preston. I want both you and Molly to live with me. But your mother has legal custody of the two of you. There just isn't anything I can do."

He had been crying so hard he was gasping for air. His body quivered in my arms. "Why did you leave us? Please, oh please, can't I move in with you?"

Preston, unlike his younger sister, whose emotions are closer to the surface, always seemed in firm control of himself. I hadn't seen him cry in years. Never before had I known him to be completely overwhelmed by his emotions. All I could do was hold him tightly, muttering soothing words the way I had when he was very young and had fallen and hurt himself.

It had been two years since I packed a few things and drove away from the house in Westchester County and moved into a dark, cramped apartment in New York City. Two painful years for all of us. But, for me at least, many of the deep emotional wounds had started to heal. I had learned to accept my life for what it was—an unintentional bachelor, a weekend father. Financially strapped, often lonely for my children, I still had managed to create a life in the city that made it possible to get up in the morning and face the day without dread.

The first weeks and months following the separation were almost unbearable. Many nights I cried myself to sleep because of bitterness and despair and guilt and loneliness. I had moved out of the house with virtually nothing ("There is no point in both of us starting all over again," my wife aptly noted). I couldn't afford to furnish the small apartment I rented and, at first, the children slept in sleeping bags on the bare living-room floor when they came in for the weekend. We ate out most of the time. I hadn't cooked for myself in fifteen years and had forgotten what little I once knew about the kitchen. Slowly, I began to buy furniture—a high-rise sofa that pulled out to make two beds so the children wouldn't have to sleep on the floor, and two small chests so they had drawers for their clothes and a place to store the games and toys we were accumulating. I bought a dining table and chairs—and a cookbook.

During those two years the children and I established a routine for our weekends together. On Friday night they were usually tired, so we stayed home and played games or watched television or just gossiped until it was time for bed. I always planned something for Saturday. A movie, a play, a baseball game, the horse show, the circus. I read the entertainment section of the Sunday paper very carefully and planned ahead. I bought them model boats and we spent long spring afternoons in Central Park at the boat pond. We played catch in Riverside Park, tossed Frisbees, took long walks along the river, visited museums—the same things all the other weekend fathers I knew did with their children.

And on Saturday night Preston and I would have what became known as our "talk." Since Molly was two years younger than her brother, she went to bed before he did, and Preston and I would go into the bedroom and just talk. He would sprawl on my bed in his pajamas and we talked about what was going on at school, what he was dreaming about for the future, about some wild invention he had concocted. Just talk. We never, before the night he begged to move in with me, talked about the divorce, about his life with his mother in the suburbs. I suppose I should have been more aware of what wasn't being discussed, of the side of his life he wasn't sharing with me in our rambling conversations. But I had not picked up any clues which would have alerted me to the depth of his unhappiness, to the apparent wretchedness of his existence.

"Can I ever live with you?" he asked when he had calmed down. His eyes were red and swollen, his face drawn.

"When you are older. We'll try to work something out when you're older. We really will. Right now, there is nothing I can do. Nothing."

"How much older?"

When the separation papers were being drawn up, I was told that judges might, just might, give some consideration to the wishes of children when they were fourteen. Before that age, the chances of a father gaining custody of his children in New York State were virtually nil.

"When you're fourteen," I told Preston. "If you still wish to move in with me when you're fourteen, we'll do everything we can. I promise you."

He had stopped crying. He blew his nose and we tiptoed into the living room, where Molly was sleeping soundly. He crawled under the covers, turned his back to me and said nothing when I kissed him good night.

The next day he was remote, sometimes sullen. Nothing I suggested—sailing the boats, playing catch, taking a walk to get out of the apartment—interested him. Most of his hostility was taken out on poor Molly, who seemed unable to do anything right from his point of view. And even as I defended Molly against his outbursts, I knew his anger, his hurt, were directed at me. I had failed him, let him down. In his moment of crisis, I had offered him little hope that things would be different.

Just before we were to leave for the five-thirty train which would take them back to their lives with their mother, Preston locked himself in the bathroom. After repeated urgings to hurry up because we might miss the train, he unlocked the door and came out. It was obvious he had been crying. The taxi ride to Grand Central Station was made in stony silence. He avoided my eyes when I kissed him goodbye on the train. Molly, knowing nothing of what had gone on the night before, seemed baffled and unhappy. She told me over and over again that she loved me, fearing, I suppose, that Preston and I had had some sort of a fight because he wasn't speaking to me. She loved her brother very much, despite the fact that he was often very rough with her, and she loved me, and she was troubled. It had happened to her before. Two people—her parents—whom she loved, no longer loved each other. She was crying silently, tears slipping down her cheeks, as the train pulled out of the station.

I couldn't face returning to the empty apartment, so I stopped off for a drink at a place where I knew a sympathetic bartender. One drink led to another, but the booze didn't help. I couldn't get the image of my son clinging to me, begging to be able to live with me, out of my mind. It was a hopeless situation. There was no chance of my gaining custody of the children. All of that had been settled and officially recorded by a judge. They were to live with their mother, I was to have alternate weekends and a month in the summer. The drinks only depressed me more, so I gave up and went back to the apartment. Later that evening, when I unrolled the "john" paper, a slip of green art paper fell to the bathroom floor. On it was written in Preston's cramped scrawl: "Dad, I love you very much. Preston."

For the first time in months I felt the sense of helplessness verging on despair I had lived through when the marriage fell apart.

Two weeks later, when I met the children at the station, it was as though nothing had happened the time they were in before. Both children embraced me, we talked in the taxi on the way to the apartment about the funny things that had happened at school, their new kitten and the trouble it was giving Molly's two caged lovebirds. I was relieved that what I had feared was a tidal wave of unhappiness had quietly slipped back down the beach and all was calm again. We went to Central Park on Saturday afternoon and sailed their boats, then saw an early movie. And when

Preston and I had our "talk" on Saturday night, we discussed such weighty problems as his design for a spaceship and where he would like to spend our vacation month together.

For the next two years the subject of his moving in with me never came up again, not directly anyway. Sometimes a remark would slip out ("When I live with you," or "When I move in"), but we never discussed it. I called several times a week to let the children know that I loved them, that I was concerned about what they were doing, to let them know I was always available. Our weekends together became more and more relaxed. I learned not to crowd too much in too short a time. I learned that our just being together, even suffering through a badly prepared dinner, was as fulfilling as an elaborate evening at a restaurant or seeing a play.

My financial condition slowly improved, and when a larger, brighter apartment opened up in my building, I took it. After nearly four years in rooms looking out on an air shaft, I had a place where my plants did not need grow lights to survive. I gave a less fortunate friend the grow lights and bought a new sofa and chairs to fill what seemed an enormous amount of space in the living room.

A month later Molly called and asked if it would be all right if she didn't come in on her regular weekend—her very best friend was having a sleepover birthday party and could she come in the following weekend. It was arranged that Preston would come in alone as planned and Molly would come in the following weekend, and we would get back on schedule after that.

After dinner Friday night, Preston helped me arrange the books on the new bookshelves and shift the furniture around. "For the first time," he said rather casually, "I feel I have a real home in the city. The other apartment was a dump."

We spent most of Saturday working on the apartment, hanging pictures, unpacking boxes I hadn't gotten around to. After dinner, we watched his favorite television program and were about to turn in when he made his announcement.

"I've thought about it. I'll be fourteen in August. I've decided to move in with you in September. I've discussed it with the counselor at school. I told him I wouldn't be attending high school up there, so I didn't have to go through all the tests and things. I'll be going to school here."

I was completely taken off guard by his statement. I tried not to show my surprise, or my sense of panic. "Have you discussed this with your mother?"

"No. This is just between you and me, okay? I've only told the counselor and my friend Bernie."

My hands were trembling slightly when I fixed myself a drink. I had completely forgotten I had promised he could move in when he was fourteen. Things had been going along so smoothly that I assumed he had made peace with the way things were.

"Have you thought it through, Preston? You'll be leaving all your friends. Changing schools. Living in an apartment in the city is a lot different from living in a big house in the country."

"I only have one friend that I care about and I can still see him. He can come in and see me. You told me I could live with you when I was fourteen."

"I told you I would do everything I could to make it possible for you to live with me. But it isn't going to be simple. You understand that, don't you?"

"I think so. That's why I'm telling you now. It's only February. That gives us several months to take care of things."

He was sitting cross-legged on the sofa, his arms spread-eagle across the back. He had grown several inches in the past couple of years. The sleeves of his flannel shirt were too short, his hair needed a trim. There was a hint of acne on his cheeks. His eyes never left mine.

"It's going to be all right, isn't it, Dad? You promised."

"It's going to be all right. Somehow, it's going to be all right. But I've got to think about it. When did you decide you wanted to move in?"

"When we talked about it before. I decided then."

"That was two years ago. You've never mentioned it since."

"I didn't think I had to."

The look in his eyes made me feel uncomfortable. He seemed to be searching my face for some clue as to my reaction. I desperately wanted to reassure him that everything was going to be fine, that in September he would pack up and leave the country and move in with me. But I wasn't at all sure it was going to happen. It certainly wasn't going to happen as easily as he assumed it would. My first impulse was to try to talk him out of it, to convince him that it was best to stay with his mother for another four years, and then he could go off to college. But my instincts warned me not to reject his plan, at least not right away. If he had been thinking about moving in for two years, I couldn't just dismiss his request. I would have to make an effort to gain custody of him—regardless of my doubts.

And I had serious doubts. It wasn't that I didn't love him. I loved both my children shamelessly. Their mother often complained that I spoiled them, which I did. Our time together was so special for me that I gave them everything I could afford. They had the best of both worlds—the quiet life in the country and the more exciting life of the city. But at the time I promised Preston he could live with me when he was fourteen, I honestly never expected him to hold me to it. I would never have promised such a thing had I thought he would simply announce two years later that he was planning to move in.

How was I going to cope with a teen-age boy in the city? My life style did not include a full-time live-in teenager. I traveled a great deal for my firm, and even when in the city, I often did not get home until one or two in the morning. I cooked for the two of them on weekends, but most of the time I picked up something at the deli on the way home. When I was alone, the dishes accumulated in the sink, the laundry never seemed to get taken out on time. I, frankly, knew nothing about the day-to-day care of a child. It had never occurred to me I would someday have to face that possibility.

Nothing in my past had prepared me for the role of full-time parent. Women took care of children. The men I knew were providers, and occasionally playmates and advisers, but they never assumed full responsibility of their children. When I had mentioned to my lawyer that I was very close to my children and would like to have custody, he told me, "Children need their mothers. It's best they live with their mother." I had accepted his advice and thought no more about it.

A sense of helplessness settled over me as I returned my son's gaze. He had made up his mind and, for him, it was as simple as that. But, for me, all I could see were storm clouds boiling up over the horizon.

"Why don't we discuss it tomorrow?" I suggested.

"Fine. But I'm going to be moving in, aren't I?"

"We'll do everything we can. We really will."

II

I am by nature a night person. My mind is clearest during the hours after midnight. The avenue in front of my apartment building is empty except for an occasional taxi heading for the garage. A stillness settles over the city. And in this stillness, the jumble of ideas I have not been able to deal with during the day begin to sort themselves out. By the time I'm tired enough to fall asleep, I've usually been able to isolate one or two of the fleeting, half-formed thoughts that have been mixed up with the other worries and to set about making plans to deal with them.

By the time I fell asleep the night following Preston's announcement, I had come to a couple of conclusions, neither of which I liked, but there seemed to be no alternatives.

The first conclusion was that his moving in would be a terrible mistake for a number of reasons. Aside from the legal and financial and emotional problems which would have to be faced if he moved in, the one over-riding conclusion was that, simply, I was not prepared to assume the full responsibility of raising a teen-age boy. The phrase I had heard for years—"Children need their mothers"—kept drifting across my mind. Like every male I know, I was brought up to believe that only women have that special instinct the raising of children requires. If I did manage to gain custody of him—and the odds were at least a hundred to one against me—what terrible price would he have to pay later in life for having walked out on his mother? It was an impossible situation. His mother was adequately caring for him. On the other hand, I knew nothing about the full-time responsibilities of child care. Somehow I would have to convince Preston he'd be better off in the long run staying in the country.

But the other side of that decision was deeply troublesome. I had promised him, without fully understanding the state of mind he was in at the time, that I would try to make the move possible when he was fourteen. If he felt I didn't want him to live with me, how would he react? Would he feel abandoned? Unwanted? Although both children had suffered a great deal when I left home four years earlier, Preston had been the one most deeply wounded. He was nearly nine then and we had, from his earliest years, a very special kind of relationship. The two of us had done many things together, we had learned to communicate on many levels. A touch, a smile, an exchange of looks. How could I make him understand he shouldn't live with me because I felt incapable of caring for him? Would he think I didn't love him if I tried to talk him out of wanting to move in? It was because I loved him that I believed he should remain with his mother. I knew I was going to have to handle the situation with as much tact and delicacy as I could muster. I would be forced to do something I had never deliberately done to him before: I would be forced to lie to him, to pretend I was doing all I could to make the move possible while finding ways to prevent it from happening. The whole idea made me feel shoddy, but if I could pull it off without his doubting my love, I would have done him a great service.

Just before dropping off to sleep that night, an idea filled my mind with the suddenness of someone snapping on a light bulb. Did I really know my own son? Regardless of how close I thought we were, I was still taken by surprise by his determination to move in. Over the years since the separation, I had spent as much time with him as I possibly could. I shared as much of my life as I could under the circumstances. I listened as attentively as I could to what he had to tell me. Yet I had not been attentive enough to pick up a single hint that would have indicated what he was thinking. I wasn't really aware of how he had changed over the past few months; not until he sat on the sofa, his dark, penetrating eyes searching my face, did I realize how grown-up he had become. I hadn't noticed the new, more assured tone in his voice, the different way he walked, the sense of independence he had developed. I was still thinking of him as my little boy. He wasn't little anymore—he was nearly as tall as I. He was already thinking of a career in medicine. He was actively interested in politics. I had discussed these things with him without noticing the changes in him, of the growing up that was happening before my unobserving eyes.

The only way I could understand my thirteen-year-old son was to try to remember who I had been at that age, to try to remember what I was thinking, where we were living, what my dreams were. What was my relationship with my parents? Were there some experiences in my youth I could use to better understand what was going on in Preston's head?

Until Preston forced me into looking backward, I hadn't given much thought to the special kind of relationship the two of us had. I can't remember ever having had a real conversation with my father at that age. I was the second of five children and the family was always together. There was no chance for me to spend time alone with him. I probably never ever tried. I do remember all of us sitting around the dining-room table doing our homework while my father read and my mother mended socks, or ironed or completed some other household chores. And when homework was finished, we went to bed. On Saturdays we all had jobs to do around the house, and on Sundays, after attending church and having midday dinner, I usually hid so I could read without being molested by my noisy siblings.

Even if my father and I had had the long, man-to-man kind of talks Preston and I did, I certainly wouldn't have asked him the same questions Preston asked me. My father told me as much as he thought I needed to know on any subject, so it would have been pointless to ask for anything more.

There was certainly no possibility that at the age of thirteen I would tell my father that I preferred to live with him. There would never have been a reason to choose between my parents. The idea of a divorce would never have crossed my parents' minds.

I grew up in small Kentucky towns, the son of a Protestant minister. Actually, he was a home missionary, working back up in the hollows of Appalachia, organizing Sunday schools in an effort to "save" the souls of the half-starved children of the mountain people. The towns we lived in were, for me, self-contained universes, completely isolated from the swirl of events of the outer, the real, world. Although the decade of the thirties was, as I now look back with some knowledge of what was going on outside my own small world, a time of great anguish for millions of Americans, it seemed not to touch us. There were children starving in the cabins up in the mountains, but children had been starving in mountain cabins long before Wall Street pulled the plug. We were affected for a few weeks when the banks were closed by President Roosevelt (my father regularly prayed for Roosevelt's soul—he was a conservative Republican and Roosevelt was responsible for the repeal of Prohibition and the recognition of Russia), but we survived without scars. Everyone had vegetable gardens, cows for milk, cold cellars full of canned food. We didn't really need cash. Our mothers made most of our clothes. All you could look forward to was a new pair of shoes . . . if you were the oldest. If you were the youngest, you got what was handed down. I think we were happy. We didn't know any other life existed. There wasn't a television set to bring into our living room pictures of people living in a style we couldn't afford. I suppose it has always been so and regrettably will always be so, that as long as there are people worse off than you, you have a sense of being superior, a sense of well-being. We were the "town people" rather than the "mountain people," who barely got through the winter, or the miners and their families who lived in dreadful, company-owned hovels and shopped at the company store. My father and many of his friends were college graduates, something that doesn't mean much now, but in the early thirties in the backwoods of Kentucky, it was a badge of rank. It set one aside. We owned a car. We were the first on our street to own a radio, and all the boys, the same ones who wouldn't acknowledge my existence during the winter, were always friendly at the end of summer because they wanted to listen to the World Series. National news on the radio featured events in faraway cities such as Lexington, Louisville or Cincinnati.

By the time Preston was thirteen, he had taken pictures of his sister leaning against a column on the Acropolis in Athens and sitting on the spot where the Delphic oracle once uttered her words of wisdom. He had watched bullfights in Madrid and shopped for souvenirs in the Casbah in Tangiers. He had lunched in the Rain Forest in Puerto Rico and listened to the wind whine through the gorges of the Grand Canyon. Greece for me at thirteen was a yellow blot on the map of my geography book. Spain was a mysterious country where Columbus found backing for his voyage off the edge of the earth. My only contact with the world beyond the mountains was an occasional slide show by Osa Johnson, who showed us pictures of the man-eating natives of Africa and the cunning and dangerous Orientals. After one of Johnson's lectures, it was comforting to return to one's bed even if you had to share it with a younger brother, and know all that evil outside world was faraway and could never touch you. "And as the sun sinks into . . ." Somehow, it wasn't the same sun that sank behind the mountain to the west every night. We knew who we were. We were safe, and simple and Christian.

In this tiny, secure island of my youth, divorce was something few children knew anything about. I had a vague idea that some married people became unmarried. Movie stars, for example. I was never allowed to go to the movies because Hollywood represented, for my father, a Babylon by the sea. The fact that an actor could commit adultery in real life and still portray innocence on the screen never got through to my father. I never knew anyone who had been divorced until I was in my twenties, and the man was a real cad. Divorce ranked above the evils of tobacco and whiskey. You could be saved from the last two, but divorce was unforgivable.

When I was in the third grade, the father of one of my friends "took off" with another woman. We all knew who she was. She wore nailpolish, rinsed her hair with henna and rouged her cheeks. She was the sort of woman our mothers warned us about. Painted ladies were "evil," the devil's disciples. Our mothers never used make-up or wore attractive dresses or high heels. Being Christian meant being dowdy. God, how dull their lives must have been. It was painful for my friends and me when we ran into the abandoned boy on the school steps the next day. It was as though my little friend had also been marked by his father's wild passion. Like father, like son. If hot passion runs in the blood of the father . . . We could find nothing to talk about with him, so we turned our backs and waited as he walked gray-faced into the classroom. A week later his mother had the good sense to ship him off to his grandparents in another part of the state, relieving all of us of the painful choice of ignoring him during recess or not walking with him on the way to school. His mother started wearing black, like a widow, and never left her house except to buy groceries or go to church, where she sat alone in a back pew.

I never liked my friend's mother very much. She was always whining about something when I went to their house to play. She had headaches and kept the blinds drawn, and the house must be as quiet as a church basement. As I look back, I certainly can't blame the man for running away with the painted lady. But at the time, we all felt sorry for her. She was an abandoned woman, the mother of an abandoned boy. The fact that this passionless creature had probably driven her husband out of the house never occurred to us. We had no understanding of sex or passion. We knew our mothers made babies—I observed the bulge in my mother's stomach three times—and that our fathers had some role to play in the whole scheme of things. We had picked up some barnyard kind of knowledge; we'd watched bulls and cows making it. And roosters and hens. But, somehow, that never really related to what might be going on in our parents' bedrooms. A cow was one thing, our saintly mother was something else. Our fathers wouldn't do that to our mothers.

Late one Saturday night, when Preston was ten, he suddenly changed the subject from spaceships to sex when we were having our talk. "Doesn't it hurt the girl?" he asked.

"Doesn't what hurt the girl?"

"When you stick your penis in. In Health Science class, they showed us. You know, the man's penis going inside the woman. Doesn't it hurt her?"

I had learned years earlier to explore Preston's questions before answering them. Why did he think making love was painful for the girl? My first impulse would have been to tell him that the sounds women make during love-making are those of ecstacy, not pain. At his age I had thought the same way he did due to an unexpected encounter in a cow pasture.

One of my daily chores was to go down to the pasture

owned by a man whose farm began where the street on which we lived ended. I would put a rope around the cow's neck and lead her to the shed at the back of our property so my father could milk her. I returned her to the pasture before going off to school in the morning.

Usually the cow (she must have had a name, for cows had names then, but I've forgotten it) would be waiting for me at the gate. But one mellow spring evening I was early and she was nowhere to be seen. A creek ran along the back of the pasture where the cows drank. The creek banks were lushly overgrown with tall grass and wild bushes. I headed for the creek across the field, carefully avoiding fresh cow droppings—I remember I was wearing my Easter shoes. As I approached I heard strange moaning sounds coming from behind a clump of bushes. Sneaking closer, I saw a pair of pants tossed over a bush. What I saw next terrified me. The daughter of the man who owned the pasture was sprawled in the deep grass, her skirt above her waist. The high school jock, a guy I feared because he liked to beat up on younger boys, was on top of her, his bare bottom rising and falling in the late afternoon light. Her moans worried me. Obviously the guy was hurting her and I wanted to help, but I was afraid to interfere. The two of them were so involved in what they were doing they hadn't heard me arrive, so I retreated as quietly as possible and hid behind the bushes. From where I was crouching, I listened as the girl's moans became little shrieks and suddenly there was an eruption of sounds, grunts from the jock, squeals from the girl. Then it was all over and the only sound I heard was the water in the creek splashing against the rocks. After what seemed an eternity the boy got up and pulled on his pants, and the two of them headed across the field toward her house, his arm around her waist. I waited until they were inside before I started looking for our cow. I knew if I told a soul what I had seen and heard, the big guy would find out and beat me to a pulp. But often, when I was alone, I would think about what I had observed by the creek and wonder what it was all about.

Some years later, when I was in the Army, I found out that the sounds I associated with sex were the sounds of pleasure, not pain. And for a long time I believed my first experience was one of a kind, an erotic night unlike anything that had ever happened before. The books written by my contemporaries have, sadly enough, proved me wrong. There seem to have been a number of older women who were lonely and more than willing to share their beds and experience with strong if inexperienced young men such as me.

Fortunately I didn't fall into the trap of answering Preston's question regarding the pain of sex based on my own experience at his age. I am quite sure his Health Science teacher did not embellish his lecture with a tape recorder. Preston's question was quite pragmatic, a matter of size and thrust. When I explained that women were equipped with the ability to give birth to children and that a child's head was much larger than a man's penis, he accepted my answer. "As a matter of fact," I found myself adding, "women enjoy having sex."

There is really very little in my growing up which sheds light on what is going on in the minds of my children. The world I knew ended with the outbreak of World War II. Things my children take for granted were nothing more than dreams or fantasies in my youth. If someone had told us that someday we would sit in front of a television set and watch live coverage of a man stepping out of a capsule onto the moon, we would have laughed. We were smart enough to know that Buck Rogers was just make-believe, like Cinderella or Peter Pan. I remember when my mother would ask me to put the card in the living-room window to inform the iceman how many pounds she needed that day. If it rained on Monday, the clothes were dried on lines in the basement. Travel meant driving forty miles to Lexington in my father's Model T Ford over roads that snaked dangerously around the mountains.

The conditions of my youth are certainly not unique. Hundreds of small towns across the country were essentially like the ones I lived in as a boy. The two central forces were the schools and the churches, both controlled by women. In my particular experience, the churches were Protestant. The ministers were male, but the control of the churches was in the hands of the women of the town. Since the ministers knew which side their bread was buttered on, they took great pains to please the ladies of the congregation. The moral tone of the town was set by the women, who also had a firm control over the schools—and the children. In my family, Mom was in complete charge. If I did something to displease my father, I was threatened with the wrath of God. My mother had a switch, and I learned to dread it much more than the wrath of God. Most of my friends' families were like mine, the only exception being the mother of a friend who was "frail" and blackmailed the entire family into waiting on her hand and foot.

One of the most important days of the year was Mother's Day. All of us dressed in our Sunday best and pinned a red flower to our jacket if our mother was alive, a white one if she was dead. There were quasi-religious rituals connected with the day, rituals which became a part of our thinking. The Sunday School lessons were always built around the glories of motherhood, with obvious references to the Virgin Mary, whose Son was to die for our sins. The near-sainthood of our own mothers wasn't missed by us. We knew our mothers were God-fearing, Christian women who devoted their lives to our well-being, and we'd better never do anything to bring shame down on their heads.

We didn't celebrate Father's Day when I was young. I wonder what sort of symbolism would have been attached to Father's Day if we had celebrated it. They couldn't very well have used Joseph. We all knew that Joseph wasn't the father of Jesus. In the pictures of the Holy Family, Joseph always seemed to be a part of the background, like the cows and sheep. He couldn't even get a room at the inn.

Most of our activities revolved around our mothers. On some special occasions we shared adventures just with our fathers, like going hunting on Thanksgiving morning. I shudder at the memory of the rabbits twitching helplessly as life drained away, their blood leaving a dark blot on the earth. Guns and physical violence are what I remember most clearly about the men I knew as a young boy. It isn't that they were violent men—certainly not my father—but there was a social pressure on them to be physical, to exert themselves, to react to the sound of shotguns exploding, of hunting dogs yapping. I remember feeling guilty that I wasn't, as the eldest male child, enjoying the hunt. All I wanted to do was to go home and get away from the dogs and the guns and the dead rabbits, but I was as trapped as my father. We were supposed to enjoy hunting.

I have only a vague memory of what the fathers of many of my friends did for a living—it wasn't really important, for I only had to deal with their mothers. And it was these women, along with my mother, who instilled in us the concepts of the sins of the flesh and the evils of adultery, and all the rest of the religious and cultural baggage I've lugged around for most of my life. It was my mother who taught me table manners, who sent me off to my piano lessons, saw to it that I felt guilty when I failed to do whatever she thought I should have done.

How was it possible for me to care for my son? I'm a man. I don't understand children. I love Preston. I love both my children but I don't know how to care for them. Somehow I had to discourage Preston from wanting to move in with me without making him feel unwanted. I felt weighted down, that Saturday night, with a burden that seemed to have no answer. I would simply have to play it by ear.

III

I make lists in the morning as a way of organizing my day. On the Monday morning following Preston's announcement, I drew up a list of steps I would have to follow if I was to resolve the problems which, on that cold February morning, appeared unsolvable. Regardless of how the issue was finally settled, someone was going to be hurt. There was no possible way of avoiding pain in the double bind confronting me. If Preston moved in, his mother would surely be crushed. If he didn't move in, he would probably be emotionally damaged. Surely a "no win" situation, regardless of what I did.

As impossible as his request was, I owed it to him to at least explore every possibility, to make an effort to clear some of the hurdles standing in the way of his moving in. Foremost, of course, were the legal hurdles. I already knew what my lawyer was going to say. Jim had known Preston's mother and me long before Preston was born. He told me, when I asked him to represent me in the divorce, that he could handle the case only so far as the initial drawing up of the separation agreement was concerned. He did not wish to become involved in a bloody battle between two of his friends and I appreciated his point of view. I also knew Jim's attitude toward custody. We had discussed it four years earlier, at the time of the divorce. Some of the ground rules had probably changed since then; we would have to see. I put "Legal advice" at the bottom of the pad. There were too many other factors to be considered before I need concern myself with the legal hassles I knew would follow any move on my part to gain custody of the boy.

At the top of the pad I put "Psychological advice." There were three troubling questions I needed answered. The first thing was why I actually dreaded the possibility that I might have to assume the responsibility of caring for my son. The second thing was why Preston had decided to leave his mother and move in with me. In our discussions I had never asked him why he wished to take such a drastic step. I didn't want him to think I was trying to pry information out of him that he did not want to volunteer. But I knew he would be open with the psychiatrist. The third, and the one that seemed the most important at the time, was the effect my not being able to gain custody would have on him. How would he react to what seemed certain failure on my part?

The second item on the top of my list was much more pragmatic. "Schools." I live in the part of New York City where the public schools appear to be training camps for juvenile delinquents. If we were to get to the point where I would have to face a judge, I couldn't very well justify taking my son out of one of the best public school districts in the country and dumping him into a school where he might have to carry a knife to protect himself. A private school was the only solution, but most of the private schools close their enrollments in January. I was certain I would find it almost impossible to find an opening at this late date. And although he was a very bright boy, his school record reflected a glaring discrepancy between potential and performance. With the competition, even if there were openings, his chances of being accepted were, at best, slim. If I couldn't place him in a decent school, then he would obviously be better off staying with his mother until he finished high school.

I didn't bother listing the various changes in life style I would have to make if he lived with me. The chances were so remote, to list them would only clutter the pad with irrelevancies, such as how on earth I was going to afford to pay for private school, rent on a larger apartment, staggering legal fees if we got to that.

The first phone call was to make an appointment for Preston and me with a psychiatrist whom I knew and trusted. In the year before my marriage completely fell apart, I had spent a number of hours on his couch trying to find out where I had gone wrong, how I should change so that some glue could be applied to the cracks in a swiftly disintegrating relationship. The fact that the marriage fell apart anyway was not his fault. By the time I reached him the situation was beyond repair. He was able, however, to help me sort out the wreckage of my life and to instill in me the emotional courage I needed to go on.

The one thing my experiences on the psychiatrist's couch made possible was the acceptance on my part that I was at least two people. One Stafford enjoys dining on a delicately prepared trout in an elegant French restaurant; the other longs to sit by the sea and read about the foundations of Tibetan mysticism. One me loves to listen to recordings of Dinu Lipatti's beautifully phrased Chopin waltzes; the other prefers the music of the mountain people I knew in my youth. The me that enjoys a properly chilled bottle of Chablis must compete in the corporate jungles; the me who would like to sit quietly and meditate must be willing to sacrifice success in the business world. For years I have had a foot on either side of the stream. I'm equally uncomfortable in the tower suites of the business world and in a hilltop Zen monastery. I belong in both and neither. This inner pendulum, swinging from one extreme to another, was certainly a contributing factor to the disintegration of my marriage.

In the beginning, mine was a better marriage than most. There were many good years, memories which offset in part the pain of the divorce. We met while we were seniors in college. I was five years older than she, a veteran of World War II. Our backgrounds couldn't have been more diverse. Vanessa belonged to an old and sophisticated northern family; I doubt that anyone in the little town I came from had ever heard of the *Social Register*. The first year we knew each other, we were just friends. She was a witty, intelligent companion; we had a lot of fun together.

I was among the men and women who were unlucky enough—or, as in my case, lucky enough—to serve in both World War II and the Korean involvement. Lucky for me because I spent the first three years of the fifties in Japan, not in the filth of a Korean foxhole. I was a public relations officer with little to do after President Truman dismissed MacArthur, a master of the delicate art of self-sell. His replacement found a glut of not particularly talented young officers who were immediately reassigned. I filled my time writing a column on music and art for a Japanese newspaper—and entertaining an exotically beautiful Japanese lady. Vanessa moved to New York. We kept in touch through occasional letters, but when the war ended and I returned to New York, I found I had misplaced her address. Ships passing in the night; not to worry.

One evening I was having a drink at the bar in Sardi's when I ran into a girl who had been Vanessa's roommate at college. Vanessa had just returned from a vacation in Europe and the two of them had taken apartments in the same building. That night we had a small college reunion, and a few months later Vanessa and I did something which was rather daring in the early fifties—we started living together. Marriage was the logical next step.

We had just settled down in a comfortable Upper West Side apartment when we decided we could no longer pay the emotional price of living in the America of 1954. McCarthyism was still spreading like a plague across the country. Old friends were no longer speaking to each other because of the political climate. It was nearly impossible to give a party without an explosion of rage from the political right or left. Several once-successful actor friends had not been employed for a long time. The spark which ignited our decision to flee was a broadcast by the late unlamented Walter Winchell, a staunch defender of the madness ripping the country apart. In the middle of Winchell's broadcast Vanessa turned off the television set. "Let's get out of here," she said. I well remember the bitterness in her voice. "You don't need this and I don't need this." Less than two months later we were on a ship bound for France.

We were booked on the U.S.S. *Constitution*, the same

ship that was to deliver another American girl to the south of France two years later. Our arrival in the Bay of Cannes was slightly less newsworthy than that of Grace Kelly, but it represented a new beginning for me. The last night at sea, the purser and chief engineer laid on a party for us, and as I stood at the rail early the next morning, I wasn't sure I shouldn't put myself out of my misery by jumping into the bay. I have never learned to deal with champagne hangovers. I watched as our luggage was tossed off the ship onto a tender which was to take us ashore. I sobered up when I saw my portable typewriter being heaved off the ship. Fortunately, it was caught. The longshoremen had missed several bags earlier and I could see parts of my typewriter spread across the deck of the tender. This trip to France was not a vacation for me. The next few months represented my big chance to write a novel, the novel most of us secretly know we have inside us.

We found a small suite of rooms in a hotel on the Left Bank in Paris. The kitchen and the bathroom were the same room—dubbed the "bathenette." The stove, which didn't work very well, was next to the bidet. The refrigerator, which refused to freeze ice cubes but did chill champagne, was at the end of the bathtub. I could soak in the tub, help myself to a split of champagne and dream of a book-club selection for my novel in progress. We dined out nearly every night with other wandering Americans—would-be writers, models, musicians. Fortunately I never tried to fool myself about our life in Paris. I knew I wasn't a budding Hemingway or Fitzgerald. The ghosts of the twenties and early thirties still wandered the narrow streets of the Left Bank, but I wasn't intimidated. Occasionally I was introduced to established American writers reduced to seeking their lost youth in the cafés of Paris, but they couldn't intimidate me either. A drunk is a drunk is a drunk, as one of the *grandes dames* of an earlier Paris crowd might have written. The only thing that did intimidate me was the city itself—the majestic buildings, the breath-taking grandeur of the avenues, the sense of history as one stands at the spot in front of Notre Dame that marks the very center of all France. I quickly learned to ignore the residents of this magnificent city; they are impossibly rude to foreigners, especially Americans. What a shame to waste such a glorious city on the French.

Late one night—or early one morning—Vanessa and I closed Charlie's Bar American, a watering hole for airline pilots and international businessmen looking for a last-minute chance for a fling before heading off to home and wife. The sun was rising over the chimneys of Paris, the traffic lights were turned off, and as I raced down the Champs Elysées toward the Place de la Concorde and the Left Bank, I was overcome with the almost dreamlike quality of my life. In a sudden surge of emotion, I felt completely at home in Paris. A little Kentucky-bred boy experiencing something never dreamed of in the untroubled days of his youth. I felt confused by the sense of happiness, but I was still young and in love and everything was possible.

In the spring of 1955 I shipped off a draft of my novel to a publishing house in New York and we boarded a ship in Marseilles which was to take us through the Suez Canal, around India, through the Strait of Malacca and up to Tokyo. Our forwarding address was in care of the editor of the Japanese newspaper I had written my weekly column for when I was in the Army. He met us at the dock in Yokohama with a handful of mail. One of the letters was from the publisher. "I wish I thought a rewrite would be helpful," the letter said, "but I doubt it. What do you want me to do with the manuscript?" Burn it, I thought. So I started over again, working well into the night, determined to succeed.

Life in Japan with an American wife was not quite the same thing as life with a Japanese lover with well-connected friends. We rented the Western half of a house in a lovely part of the city and settled down to a round of embassy parties and trips to the mountains with people I had known before. In 1955 Japanese officials weren't particularly fond of Americans. The two-month visa we had been issued in Paris, with the understanding that we could stay as long as we wished, was extended twice, but the second extension was the last. So, after six months, we boarded an Italian ship for Europe. As we sailed out of Yokohama I wondered if I would ever return to the country which had made so profound an impression on my mind and soul. I loved the mountains, the cherry blossoms, the temples, the art, the gentleness of the people, the serenity of their religion.

Before leaving Tokyo, I purchased a three-volume edition of Somerset Maugham short stories for shipboard reading. It was as though he had been writing about the people we met on our way to and from Japan. The stiff-upper-lip English couple with a hyphenated name from Kuala Lumpur who boarded the ship in Singapore. They were still under the impression that the sun had never set on the British Empire and treated the Filipino stewards with hauty condescension. And the Pakistani who had been an ambassador in Peking, traveling with his sari-clad wife, three children and four servants—and a gut-ripping hatred for the

English for the way they handled the partition of India. And the sad-faced Dutch consul from Kobe, Japan, who had "gone native" and was being recalled. Then there was the silly young American diplomat on his way to a post in Laos who created a scandal by having an affair with the wife of an American banker, forcing the poor man to cut short his voyage and fly home from the next port of call a sad, broken man.

Our ship docked at Genoa. After a short visit with friends in Bolsano in the Italian Tyrols we returned to Paris, where I put the finishing touches on the revision of what I thought was a comic novel dealing with the Korean War. The second version of the book was received with the same lack of enthusiasm as the first. Our money was running out. It was time to face reality. We packed and headed for New York.

Behind us were two wonderful years. We had made love during an earthquake in Tokyo, danced on the aft deck of a pacquet boat plowing through the mirror-smooth waters of the Red Sea, nearly missed our ship in Singapore because we danced too long at the Raffles Hotel, sipped gin and tonics on the sun deck of a ship docked in Saigon and watched with morbid fascination as mortar shells flattened the city of Cholon, watched a camel caravan plod along faster than our ship as we crept through the Suez Canal. On our way to Paris from Italy, both of us acted out a childhood fantasy by making wild love on the Orient Express as it rumbled through the tunnels under the Alps.

Two great years, followed by four good years in New York. After a couple of false starts I finally ended up at one of the television networks doing program promotion. I wrote those brief, mostly meaningless announcements at the end of programs urging the viewer to stay tuned for what was coming up next. We had season tickets to the New York Philharmonic, attended gallery openings, gave, and were invited to, interesting dinner parties, kept abreast of what was new in the theater.

But after six years of marriage, a decision had to be made. Were we going to live the lives of dilettantes—I completely gave up any idea of being a writer—or were we going to settle down and have a family and live the life other people thought worthwhile? Vanessa made the decision. She wanted to have children. I had serious reservations. Even at the age of thirty-five I still wondered if there wasn't more to life than being a parent. I really didn't want to be burdened with the responsibility of being a father. But I loved Vanessa and wanted her to have the sort of life she wished. The life she wanted included children.

On August 24, 1960, my wife gave birth to a boy, the first son of the first son, etc. There were tears of joy in my voice the night I called Vanessa's family and mine to announce the birth of Preston Conover Stafford. It had happened. I was a father. Twenty-six months later I became the father of Mary Clay Stafford, a beautiful little girl. The die was cast. We gave up our subscription to the New York Philharmonic, went to fewer and fewer gallery openings, saw fewer and fewer plays, entertained less and less. When Preston was approaching six, we started looking for a house in the suburbs. By the time he was six we had found one which we couldn't afford any more than our friends could afford the houses they had bought in their flight from a city they could no longer deal with. Then it began—that slow but sure disintegration of a marriage.

I'm not very good around the house. I don't like replacing broken windows or repairing basement floors or painting bedroom ceilings. I hate standing on station platforms in the snow, waiting for a train that will puff into the station an hour late. There are much more interesting things to do than rake leaves, or trim bushes or cut the grass. I loved my wife and adored my children, but I began to see less and less of them. The pendulum began to swing the other way, that pendulum which reminded me there was more to life than making it in the corporate world, of worrying about raises, promotions, lunching with people who count. But I was trapped, hopelessly trapped in the suburban existence of having drinks with a neighbor who never talked of anything but the new addition he wanted to build on his house or the one who was planning to dig a new septic tank. My days were dominated by train schedules, nonfunctioning dishwashers, broken clothes dryers, outrageous tax increases—and a bored, housebound wife. The end of the marriage was, certainly, only a matter of time. But I didn't have the courage to break it off. I guess the male is often much more pragmatic than the female. We seem to tolerate situations long after any spark of life has faded. I later learned I was not unique. Seven out of eight divorces are initiated by women.

At the end of the evening when I took Vanessa out to dinner to celebrate our fifteenth wedding anniversary, she asked for a divorce. At first I didn't take her seriously. With her usual wit, she had chosen the most unlikely moment for such a statement. I thought she was kidding. "The best anniversary present you can give me is a divorce," she said over brandy.

"Can't I have a year's option?" I quipped.

"No."

So it was over. We returned home, paid the baby-sitter and had a nightcap in the study. The children were asleep in their rooms upstairs. We were alone, two people who had lived together for nearly sixteen years. There was no point in discussing it further. Vanessa had made up her mind. I moved into the guest room, crawled under the covers engulfed by a sense of failure and despair, and fell into a restless, dreamless sleep. There were many things which had to be settled, but like Scarlett O'Hara, I would think about that tomorrow—and as it turned out, tomorrow and tomorrow and tomorrow.

IV

"You can't afford to take him," Bill warned me. "Last year Helen offered to let me have Jimmie; the kid wanted to move in, but I just couldn't swing it. Of course, Helen wanted me to continue paying her support payments even though I'd be feeding the kid."

"How could she expect you to pay support when the boy was with you?"

"Claimed she'd need the money to keep the house going. All that broad thinks about is money."

Bill and Helen were divorced before I met him. He was one of the pathetic souls who signed away his future when the marriage broke up. For reasons I will never understand, his lawyer had talked him into agreeing to pay Helen 40 percent of his gross salary—before deductions—for the rest of his life. Recently his accountant had warned him not to take a new, better-paying job. The raise would put him in a new tax bracket and, coupled with the increase in payments to Helen, he would have less to live on than he did. It was as though his life had stopped all forward movement at the age of forty-eight. To advance in his company was really a backward step financially. I couldn't help feeling sorry for him. His ex-wife's revenge was destroying him.

"Why did she offer to let you have the boy?"

"He's nothing but trouble. I don't think I could have cared for him even if I had the money for a bigger apartment, school fees, all the rest of it. She's done a damn good job of turning both the kids against me. Do you know how to take care of Preston? Have you ever really taken care of your children?"

I had to admit that I hadn't. For a couple of months I had been responsible for taking care of him, but that was years before, when he was born. When we brought him home from the hospital, we were told he had a minor staphylococcus infection. There were a couple of small pustules on his stomach, but we weren't to worry. Newborn babies seem to throw off infections quite easily. The doctor was right, but what he hadn't warned us about was that one of us could become infected. Vanessa was breastfeeding the baby and within a week she had to be rushed back to the hospital with a fever topping 105 degrees. She was seriously ill with a new virulent strain called Australian staphylococcus. The strain had made its way through England and had just been identified by doctors in America. The usual drugs could not combat the infection. English medical researchers had developed a successful drug, but the supply was limited. Fortunately Vanessa's general good health pulled her through. She remained in the hospital ten days. When she returned home, however, she was still contagious because the lanced breast containing the infection had not healed and continued to drain. Under no condition was she to touch the child, or anything he might come in contact with, until she was completely healed. That took more than two months.

I hadn't been around infants since my baby sister appeared in the world nearly twenty-five years before. I knew that you had to hold them in such a way that you supported their heads; I knew you burped them after feeding. I had never changed a diaper or bathed a child. I felt totally helpless, but I had few options. There was no one on either side of the family I could call on to do the job, no maiden aunts, no available grandmothers. I would simply have to learn to take care of him.

Through our doctor I found a registered nurse who was available five days a week, from nine in the morning until six in the evening. She turned out to be a warm, practical woman who genuinely loved children. She arrived promptly at nine every morning, taking over as I rushed off to the office. She was ready to leave when I returned home at six. And from six at night until nine in the morning, my son was my sole responsibility. The nurse would mix enough formula to get me through the night, and she taught me how to change him, powder him, oil his bottom, burp him. After I got over my panic I found it was relatively easy to take care of a baby. The getting up in the middle of the night was exhausting—I often used my lunch hour to take a nap on the sofa in my office—but there were no crises during those months I couldn't handle. On the weekends I bathed him and took him to the park in his pram, put his clothes through the washing machine, talked with the man who arrived every Saturday morning with the next week's supply of fresh diapers, prepared the formula, sterilized the bottles. There was a lot to get done in a day, but I became organized enough to cope with it.

The reaction of my friends at the office was most sympathetic. The women, all single, worried about the welfare of the boy. It was inconceivable that a man could care for a very young infant. My male colleagues, most of them married and fathers, felt sorry for me. They had "helped out" when their children were young, but none of them seemed particularly fond of child care. "I hope never to smell a diaper pail again for as long as I live," one friend told me over lunch. "They're nothing more than little animals until they are three or four years old."

During the period of Vanessa's illness I knew that my having full control of the nursery was a temporary thing. The job was essentially Vanessa's, I was merely filling in until she could take over. There were moments during those weeks, however, which I still remember with a great deal of pleasure. The feel of his tiny fingers clutching one of mine as he sucked his bottle. The smell of his skin, not yet polluted with junk food and cigarette smoke and beer. The gurgling sounds he made when his bottom was dry and his stomach full, and he was lying on his back kicking his legs and waving his arms about. I remember most fondly the feeling of his tiny body against mine, his head snuggled against my neck and the sense of deep satisfaction that this beautiful, fragile creature was actually my son, a part of me. Surely women who carry a child inside them for months have this same satisfying experience, but I have never heard men say they felt a surge of love when holding their child. I suppose we think such sentiments unmanly—or maybe they really didn't feel toward their child the way

I felt, even at three in the morning, when I walked around the nursery with a drowsy infant held against my chest waiting for that final burp before putting him back in his crib. As I look back on those weeks it seems such a short span of time in my life, and yet, such an important span.

When the doctor announced that Vanessa was totally free of infection, I turned over my control of the nursery with a feeling of relief. I was physically exhausted. A demanding job plus the caring for my newborn son had taken its toll. A month later, while on a business trip to California, I came down with a roaring case of the mumps (which, by the way, had to be diagnosed over the phone with my doctor in New York—doctors in California head for the golf courses and beaches on Wednesday afternoon). Four weeks later I ended up in the hospital with pneumonia.

Somehow, all of us survived the arrival of our first child. Two years later, when we were expecting the second child, we were better prepared. We changed hospitals to avoid the old infection, and we engaged a fantastic German nannie who moved in to care for Preston the day Vanessa went to the hospital and stayed on for another six weeks to get us through the roughest time of early parenthood. Young Mary Clay lived in style for the first few weeks of her life, and her mother and I were able to sleep through the night without worrying about warming bottles or changing diapers.

After the period of having to take care of Preston, I was never responsible for the children for more than a few hours at a time—until the divorce. I did what most fathers do. I took them with me to the hardware store on weekends, or gave them lunch if their mother wanted to take a nap. After we moved to Westchester County I always arrived home long after they had been bathed and given their supper. I kissed them goodbye in the morning as I dashed for the train station. I loved my children very much, but I couldn't spend a lot of time with them. We had moved to the suburbs for the sake of the children—children need grass and trees, we were reminded over and over. I certainly didn't know then that grass and trees are a poor substitute for a father who is seldom around. Had I known, I would never have joined the lemmings who rush down into Grand Central Station every evening to catch a train which will get them home just before the children are tucked into bed.

The spring following my separation was so hectic that I completely forgot to make plans for the month I was to have with the children. It was late May before it occurred to me that August was only two months away. I couldn't possibly expect the children to spend their vacation in my hot, dark apartment. I frantically began calling real estate agents to see if there was a beach cottage available I could afford. At that late date the only places being offered were prohibitively high, and I simply couldn't swing it.

"Why don't you take them to Puerto Rico?" a friend suggested when I told him about my predicament. "I took my daughter there last summer. I'll give you the name of the man I rented the apartment from. It's on Luquillo Beach and completely furnished. You'll need a car to get around, but other than that, you'll be fine. It's a lot cheaper taking an apartment than staying in a hotel."

God sometimes takes care of fools. The apartment was still available at a price I could afford, there was space on the airlines on the date I wanted, and I could rent a VW on a monthly basis. After all the arrangements had been made, I had time to get cold feet. What in heaven's name was I going to do with the children for a whole month at Luquillo Beach? We had spent a week together in the spring during their school break, but we had movie theaters, restaurants, museums. Would there be children around who spoke English? Other than swimming, was there anything for the children to do?

"For God's sake, take a woman along," this same friend insisted. "How old are they?"

"Seven and nine. The girl is seven and the boy nine."

"Don't you know someone you can stand having around for a month? You're going to need a woman to care for the children. Especially the little girl. I took Frannie with me. She was great with my daughter."

Unfortunately, I had been so absorbed in my sense of failure as a husband that I hadn't got to know a woman I could possibly invite for a month's vacation in Puerto Rico —knowing she was being asked along to act as nursemaid for my children. The three of us would just have to make do.

I had forgotten how hot and humid the islands can be. A blast of hot air hit us as we got off the plane in San Juan. By the time we had claimed our luggage, picked up our rented car and stuffed it with all our luggage, there wasn't a dry thread on me. We went shopping for groceries, and it was late in the afternoon by the time we reached the apartment complex on the beach. "I'll leave the keys for you," the man I rented the apartment from had told me. I assumed he meant at the building. I found the manager's office and asked for the keys. He didn't have them. It seemed the owner had left them with the rent-a-car people —the other rent-a-car people. The manager of the building spoke about as much English as I spoke Spanish, but slowly we worked things out. He had master keys and would let me have a set until I could make other arrangements. By the time we got all our luggage and the bags of groceries up to the apartment, it was dusk. I grilled hamburgers, then dug out the children's pajamas, and they were soon in bed, exhausted from the day.

I fixed myself a cold drink and collapsed in a chair on the balcony overlooking the ocean. The scouts for the *Michelin Guide* would have assigned a red rocking chair to the apartment complex. It was certainly "a quiet and secluded situation." The moonlight glistened on the sea, the palm fronds rustled in the soft breeze. The only sound I heard was the waves softly breaking on the beach. Thirty days and thirty nights in a quiet and secluded situation.

The days just before leaving New York had been hectic. I had never taken off for a month before and there were things that had to be finished before I left. I did remember to buy a collection of Sherlock Holmes stories and a couple of Nancy Drew mysteries to read to the children. I had also bought sun-tan lotion and enough toothpaste and shampoo to last the month. But there wasn't a television set or a radio. We hadn't brought any of the games the children liked to play. What in God's name was I going to do to entertain the children for a whole month? I realized, as I watched the moon's reflection on the water, that I should have taken my friend's advice. I should have brought along a woman to help take care of the children.

The next morning I fixed scrambled eggs and toast. "They're too mushy," Molly said of the eggs. (At the age of six, Mary Clay had announced that she wanted to be called Molly.) The toaster insisted on turning one slice of bread after another into slivers of charcoal. The milk smelled funny. We gave up on breakfast and headed for the beach.

We were the first to arrive. The children dropped their towels on the sand and dashed into the surf. They were fearless, diving into the waves, coming up gasping for air and diving back under again. I watched them with mounting concern. I have an insane fear of drowning and there was no lifeguard. If something should happen, an undertow, a wave too big for them to deal with, there was very little I could do. I didn't want to instill fear in them as it has been instilled in me, but at the same time, I didn't relish the idea of standing on the beach watching one of my children being washed out to sea. Not on our first day of vacation.

By midmorning the sand was littered with beach towels, the surf with tanned, screaming children. I settled down to read, but it was difficult to concentrate. Dripping youngsters were constantly dashing up and down the beach, kicking sand on my blanket. It was obvious that the relationship between the adults on the beach and the uninhibited children was an undeclared war. The mothers were shouting commands, the children gleefully ignoring them. "Don't throw sand on your sister," a mother screamed as a young boy picked up another handful and dumped it on his sister's head. "Stop dripping all over me," another complained, grabbing a towel to protect a bathing suit obviously not designed for anything more than sunbathing. Many of the women wore scarfs in an attempt to disguise the fact that they had their hair up in curlers.

It was nearly lunchtime before I became aware that I

was the lone male in charge of children on the beach. There were couples without children, but no fathers watching over their brood. Except me. I sat on my blanket, pale as a refugee from a Soviet labor camp, feeling quite out of place and hot and sweaty. The children and I had had enough sun for the first day, so I began to stuff our suntan lotion and my book into the beach bag. Then I heard my daughter's voice behind me.

"My mother isn't with us. We're divorced."

"You mean, your parents are divorced," a woman corrected her.

"Yes. We're divorced. I'm here with my father."

"That's too bad. But everything will be all right. You'll see."

Molly's statement sent a chill down my spine. She had insisted on using the collective "we" when discussing her parents' divorce. It was the first time either of the children had even mentioned the divorce in my presence. And she obviously thought the family was divorced, not just her parents. My small-town Kentucky background made me feel guilty and ashamed.

I turned around. Molly was talking with a woman I hadn't noticed before. She was apparently the mother of one of the girls Molly had met in the surf. She was as brown as a chestnut, with short-cut graying hair, and she was wearing a bathing suit she must have purchased before she went off her diet.

When Molly caught my eye, she called to me, "Dad, this is Tina's mother. Tina's my new friend. She comes here every summer."

"You're down here alone with the children?" Tina's

mother asked. Her voice had that distinctive quality of a person who was accustomed to giving orders and having them obeyed. "How long are you staying?"

"A month." It didn't seem necessary to answer her first question. I began folding the blanket and gathering up our gear.

"You'd better watch the children. They've had enough sun for the first day. You shouldn't be using that lotion. It isn't strong enough. The sun is fierce down here."

"I've noticed. We're heading back to the apartment."

"Whose place have you rented?"

I told her and made a move to leave.

"Not a bad place. Small, but with just you and the children, big enough, I suppose. What on earth are you going to do with the children for a whole month? Can you cook?"

"Some."

"Tina likes Molly. Why don't the three of you come up to my apartment for dinner? They can probably stand a good meal."

"Can we, Daddie?" Molly said. She was holding Tina's hand. On her first day, she had found a friend. Preston was standing nearby drying his hair with a sandy towel, his face a mask. I had no idea what he was thinking.

There was no real reason to turn down the invitation, so we settled on a time. On the way back to the apartment, Molly was chattering about her new friend and what fun she was going to have. Preston closed the conversation by announcing he thought Tina was a drip. During my first morning in Puerto Rico I had won one—Molly had a friend—and lost one—Preston didn't like her. As it turned out, the vacation was all downhill from that morning on.

Preston had been most perceptive. Tina did indeed turn out to be a drip, which probably accounted for her mother's haste to cement the relationship between the two girls. By the third day I noticed that Molly was the only child on the beach who would have anything to do with the sad-faced waif. After a week, even a very tolerant Molly began avoiding the poor child.

Tina's mother was in a class by herself. She knew how to play on my insecurities with the skill of a master craftsman. Within twenty-four hours every mother in the twenty-storied building knew there were two young children on the third floor in the lone care of a male. My daily shopping list was drawn up for me on the beach. I was given lessons on how to fold the children's permanent-press clothing, how to deal with the sand that accumulated in the bathtub drain, where to purchase the best and freshest fruit, how to cook fish, which the children despised.

We were invited to dinner at someone's apartment at least three times a week. I hated cooking and frankly appreciated the luxury of sitting on the balcony watching the sunset while someone else prepared dinner. But roses have thorns. I was never allowed to forget something I already knew only too well. Everything I tried to do, from putting Molly's hair up in braids to treating a sunburn had the distinctive mark of an amateur, a male trying to do a job he was not qualified to do. My two were most cooperative. They never complained when the steaks I grilled were overdone, the vegetables underdone. After they were in their pajamas, we sat on the balcony and I read a chapter from a Nancy Drew book for Molly and a Sherlock Holmes adventure for Preston. On the nights we weren't invited out, we often went down to a restaurant on the square in the village of Luquillo and had cheeseburgers. Near the end of the month I gave up cooking entirely. Sweeping the sand out of the apartment, changing the beds, doing the laundry, washing dishes had gotten to me. We had sandwiches for lunch and we either went to some apartment in the building or ate dinner out. I don't think their health was seriously impaired by the experience of living with their father for a month. However, I did feel like one of the walking wounded by the time we got off the plane at Kennedy Airport on August 31.

One would have thought I had learned my lesson in Puerto Rico, but I blundered into the same thing the next year. I had to go to California on business during the summer and decided, for reasons my creditors will understand, to combine my trip with the month's vacation with the children. I sublet, through a friend, an apartment on Venice Beach in the Los Angeles area. The beach on the Pacific was much different from the one in Puerto Rico. My two were often the only children battling the heavy surf, and the bathing suits the ladies were wearing, what there was of them, were certainly oceangoing. There were also interesting things to do in the area—visit Disneyland, Marineland, the *Queen Mary* docked at Long Beach. But I had gotten myself into the same rut. Dinners with the meat done fifteen minutes before the vegetables, mornings when there were no clean towels or shorts, endless hours in the supermarket. After two weeks I gave up and loaded the children into the car and drove down to San Diego. We spent a week at a lovely motel on the beach (our room had a stove and a refrigerator, which I only used to prepare breakfast). We then flew over to Arizona to stay with a generous friend for a week before returning to New

York. Because of the last two weeks, the children rated the vacation much higher than the one we had spent in Puerto Rico, and I was in a much more relaxed mood when the plane put down in New York at the end of the month.

During the Christmas holidays following the trip to California, the children and I held a family caucus. What would they like to do next summer? Take a beach cottage? Rent a Winnebago and tour Canada? What? The vote was three to nothing against renting a cottage.

"You hate cooking," Molly observed.

"Would it be possible to go to Europe? A friend of mine went to Greece with his dad and stepmother last summer," Preston suggested.

Europe had never occurred to me. But why not? And I had never been to Greece. The children were old enough to benefit from a tour of the classic ruins of a civilization which influenced all Western thought. We immediately began collecting tourist brochures and flight information. Since they could travel half fare, the cost of transportation wasn't as much as I thought it would be. By April I had renewed my passport, secured passports for the children and made airline reservations.

The vacation was a total success. After four days in Athens we took a bus tour of the major historical sites which, even for me, were merely names out of some textbook. Preston raced Molly in the stadium in Olympus; we tramped through museums and climbed mountains to inspect ancient temples. After the bus tour we settled down on the island of Rhodes for the remainder of the month. Long, relaxed days of cloudless skies and gentle waves—and terrible food. But I didn't have to shop for it, prepare it or clean up. The laundry came back ironed and neatly folded. Concerned chambermaids took pity on a male traveling alone with two children and took particularly good care of us. Other tourists we met thought us quite strange. In one hotel we made friends with an American woman traveling with her two daughters—and no one thought she was doing something daring. Women could travel with children, but a male . . . There were moments I agreed with the prevailing attitude, but living in hotels was certainly better than trying to cope with an apartment somewhere.

After Greece, there was no longer any question of what to do with that special month the children and I shared each summer. All we had to decide was which country to visit next. Spain won.

After five days in Madrid doing the usual things tourists do in Spain—watching a bullfight, tramping through the Prado and the Royal Palace, and dining in delightful restaurants in the Plaza Mayor—we picked up our rental car and took off, without hotel reservations, for a tour of the country. Finding a hotel room in Spain in August is not unlike one of Cinderella's stepsisters trying to shove her foot into the glass slipper. It became a game. Spaniards are very *macho*, so I played on the sympathies of the men behind the hotel desks. I was a male traveling alone with two tired children. No self-respecting Spaniard would put himself in such a compromising situation, and I'm sure out of pity for me, a room in a totally booked hotel would be provided. I never allowed myself the luxury of worrying about the people who arrived after we did with what they thought was a confirmed reservation. Preston's twelfth birthday was celebrated in Málaga, followed by a quick trip to Tangiers, then back to New York. Another highly successful vacation.

The month the children and I spent together became the centerpiece of our year. We had decided to tour Spain over the Thanksgiving holiday following our return from Greece. We had already settled on Yugoslavia for the next summer when Preston announced that February evening that he was moving in.

"Will my moving in change our vacation plans?" he asked on Sunday morning. "I'm really looking forward to going to Yugoslavia."

I hadn't slept very well. It was raining. August was a long way away. There were too many things to think about without worrying about whether or not we could afford Yugoslavia. If he were to move in with me, it would certainly affect vacation plans. His move would have a dramatic effect on everything I was planning for the future, but I couldn't share that with him.

"Don't worry about it," I told him. "I'm sure we'll get to Yugoslavia this summer."

V

I swore Preston to secrecy. If his mother knew he wanted to live with me, she would be deeply hurt. There was no reason to put a further strain on the relationship between them. Since it was unlikely I would ever be granted custody, I wanted his life with his mother to be as comfortable as possible. The psychiatrist would help Preston adjust to living with his mother and within a few weeks this would all be behind us.

I made the appointment for the next Saturday morning the children were coming in. So that Molly wouldn't wonder why Preston was seeing a psychiatrist, I arranged for a friend to take her shopping for a new dress. We were to meet later at a restaurant for lunch.

"What do I say to him?" Preston asked in the taxi on the way across town.

"He knows why you're seeing him. I've talked with him about it. Just be open and honest. Tell him the reasons you want to move in."

I had explained over the phone as much as I could. I really didn't understand Preston's reasons for making such a drastic change in his life. It wasn't as though his mother was an irresponsible drunk, or that she beat him or physically mistreated him in any way.

Preston was immediately shown into the doctor's inner office when he arrived. I settled down in the waiting room. I couldn't concentrate on the back issues of *The New Yorker* spread out on the tables. I kept emptying and refilling my pipe. I felt as if I were buckled into my seat on a plane waiting at the end of a runway for clearance to take off. I don't mind flying once I'm in the air, but I'm close to panic just before takeoff.

After what seemed an endless hour, the door opened and Preston came out. His eyes were red from crying; he was still dabbing at them with a tissue. "The doctor wants to talk to you," he said and sank down on a sofa.

"Are you all right?"

"Sure. I'll wait for you here."

There were butterflies in my stomach as I went in. I couldn't tell from Preston's expression what he was feeling. I desperately hoped he understood why it was best that he stay with his mother.

"That's quite a boy. If I had a son, I would want him to be like Preston."

"Do you think he understood?"

"Understood what?"

"What we discussed on the phone. That he should remain in the country until he finishes high school."

"Under no circumstance should he remain in the country. He must move in with you, and the sooner the better."

It was like a moment in a dream when you're slipping deeper and deeper into the water and there is nothing to grasp hold of.

"But I can't care for him here in the city," I protested.

"Of course you can. Preston worships you. You can't let him down. You can take care of him."

"Did you tell him that he should move in?"

"I simply told him we wanted to make sure that it was a wise move before we did anything else. Have you talked with your lawyer?"

"I've been waiting until Preston talked with you. I had thought you would feel he should stay with his mother." Whatever I had thought was obviously wrong. Very quietly, as though speaking to a young child, the doctor explained that it wasn't a question of which of us was a better parent. Preston's mother and I were simply different kinds of people, we reacted to life in different ways. In his earlier years Preston had identified more closely with me. I was, as the doctor patiently explained, Preston's primary parent.

"But she's a good mother."

"That isn't the point. At this stage in his life he needs to be with you."

"What will happen to him if I can't gain custody? There's a real possibility I can't get him."

"Problems. Lots and lots of problems."

"But isn't it possible for him to adjust to his life up there? Maybe if I saw him every weekend instead of alternate weekends . . . I'm sure his mother would agree to that, for a while anyway, until we get over the immediate problem. I'm on the phone two or three times a week. I'm always in touch. I haven't withdrawn from his life."

The doctor was adamant. Spending every weekend with me would be better than the current arrangement, but no real solution to the problem. Preston wanted to live with me full time. I tried to explain that I was worried that Preston thought life with me was going to be one long party. In the four years since the separation I had been the goodie box, the giver of fun things, provider of exotic vacations, baseball tickets. If he lived with me full time, I would have to insist on homework being done, all the routine chores of a fourteen-year-old's existence. The doctor never budged from his original position.

"I have no idea how his mother is going to react to this. She won't want to give him up."

"You'll have to appeal to her very real concern for the boy's welfare."

"Legally I haven't a leg to stand on. I don't know a single father who has custody of his children. Judges won't turn a child over to a man. You know that."

"Do they really want custody? Your friends?"

"No, actually not. I suppose they feel the same way I do. I'm not sure I can pull this off—I mean, caring for him if I should get custody."

"You've got to make the effort for the sake of the boy."

My carefully planned escape hatch had been slammed shut in my face. The doctor was firmly on Preston's side.

"What about Molly? What is she going to think if Preston moves out?"

"Let's cross one bridge at a time. You must understand how important it is for the boy to be with you. I'll do all I can to help you."

My knees were a little wobbly when I returned to the waiting room. "Ready for lunch?"

Preston got to his feet and took my hand. "I feel a lot better. I'm really hungry."

Neither of us said anything about what had just happened as we walked the few blocks to the restaurant where Molly and my friend were waiting.

"Want to see my new dress?" Molly asked.

"Let's wait until we get home. What would you like to eat?"

My friend caught my eye. There was nothing I could tell her in front of Molly. I shrugged and ordered her a drink. Preston was highly animated and laughed easily. It was as though nothing was more important to him than the story he was telling my friend of one of the practical jokes he had pulled on a schoolmate. What he didn't realize was that the drama had not come to an end with his visit to the doctor. In reality, it had only just begun. I found it difficult to concentrate on the conversation bouncing around the lunch table.

The children walked before my friend and me out of the restaurant. "What happened?" she asked in a whisper.

"The doctor thinks it is imperative that Preston move in."

"Jesus. Best of luck."

"I'm going to need a lot more than luck."

On the surface, the remainder of the weekend was no different from the many weekends preceding it. We went to a movie in the afternoon and I broiled a steak for dinner. Molly was caught up in Preston's carefree mood and the two of them laughed and joked a great deal. I was the only one who felt depressed, but they didn't appear to notice it.

After Molly went to bed Saturday night, I warned Preston that there were still many obstacles we would have to deal with before he could move in. "I'll have to get you into a school and it may be too late. You understand that, don't you?"

"Sure." He seemed almost unconcerned. Nothing I said dampened his high spirits.

On Monday morning I called a friend who had written a book on the private schools in New York City. He was free and agreed to meet me for lunch.

"I think you're in trouble," he warned me. It was already mid-March, and most good schools, especially for the ninth grade, were filled by the beginning of February. We went down a list of schools he felt would best meet Preston's needs and narrowed it down to two. "Start here," he said, "and if they are full, call me and we'll expand the list. What are you going to do if you can't get him into a school?"

"I haven't the vaguest idea."

One of the main reasons for moving to the suburbs years before had been that I wanted my children to attend public schools. Now, eight years later, I was caught up in the private-school hassle other friends had gone through.

"The middle class pays a terrible price to stick it out in New York," my friend told me. "The upper class can afford private education. The lower class can get scholarships if their children are bright. We're the ones who are squeezed. Move out of the city or forget about summer vacations."

"And most everything else. I don't know how I'm going to swing this."

"Like the rest of us. You'll manage to find the money. What I would worry about is having to take care of the boy. I couldn't care for my two without Betty."

"There is still a possibility I won't have to take care of

Preston. I haven't talked to my lawyer yet. I'm still trying to see if I can get him in a school. If I can't, then . . . we'll have to see."

My friend was right. When I called the school he recommended as first choice, the admissions director informed me the class was full. When she asked me why I was applying so late, I told her that although I didn't yet have custody, I was going to make an effort if I could get him into a school. My tale of woe was, depending on how you look at it, most effective. "I always squirrel away a place for situations such as yours," she said. "I'll send you an application." I wasn't sure that was good or bad news.

She also told me I had to have Preston take a number of tests which all private schools used to select candidates. That wasn't going to be easy to arrange. The testing bureau did not administer private tests on weekends, and the regularly scheduled sessions didn't fall on a weekend Preston would be in town. To have him tested by his school counselor was risky. I still felt it was best that his mother not find out what was going on until I had all my ducks lined up. When I explained to Preston's counselor the need for secrecy, he became very evasive. Since I did not have legal custody of my son, the school really couldn't become involved. For the first time it really struck home that I had no rights as a father. Obviously I knew he was in his mother's custody, he lived with her, she ran his day-to-day life, but it had never occurred to me that he was legally her property. I was without any rights other than visitation rights. I felt my anger rise. He was my son, and for the first time I became determined to exert my paternal rights. I got in touch with the attorney retained by the

Board of Education and explained my problem as calmly as possible. To my surprise he agreed that I could request the school to administer the tests—without informing the boy's mother. I also had the right to have the school forward his academic records to the admissions director in the city.

Within three weeks my second line of defense had been breached. Preston did very well on the tests, and even though his grades left a lot to be desired, the admissions director took into account the boy's emotional state and gave him the slot she had squirreled away.

I was left with the last item on the list I had made—the legal obstacle. The brush with the school counselor had clarified my own thinking. The ownership of my son which I had signed away so casually four years earlier stuck like a bone in my throat. Had I not become involved, at Preston's urging, in trying to make it possible for him to live with me, the full implication of the whole child-custody situation would never have occurred to me. I had not fought for custody because I assumed it was best the children remain in their home, stay in the same school. The fact that I had actually signed away all rights as a father had not been discussed. I was thinking in terms of living arrangements, not legal rights. Since there had never been any serious friction between the children's mother and me, the larger implications had never been tested. I had always sent my checks on time. I had never been denied my visitation rights. The children had never been urged not to see me, as had happened to a number of my friends. But legally, they were no longer my children. There was no point being angry with the school counselor, he was only following the rules. I was the person responsible for the situation to exist in the first place.

As much as I dreaded a legal confrontation, I was now sufficiently angry with myself to make the move. The thought of what a friend of mine went through sent chills down my spine. Custody battles have to be the most demeaning, emotionally destructive clashes anyone can possibly experience. I stood idly by when my friend went to court four times trying to wrest his daughter from the grasp of a mentally deranged woman, each time walking away a broken and sadder man. I wasn't a father then and had no understanding of why he persisted, year after year, to tear himself to emotional shreds because he wanted custody of his child. His relationship with his former wife was reduced to raw hatred. His career was seriously affected. For six months, while his ex-wife was actually in a mental institution, he had his daughter with him. But when the doctors released the woman, she immediately regained custody. The judge literally ignored the evidence that the woman was suicidal and totally incapable of caring for herself, let alone a seven-year-old. That horrible legal myth of a natural mother's right to her child had no real meaning for me then. My friend's misery was finally resolved when his ex-wife sent the little girl off to school one morning, then took the elevator to the roof of her building and jumped off. Yet, for four years, no judge would grant the father custody of the child.

What chance did I have? If Preston's mother decided to fight, she would undoubtedly win. She had taken good care of the children, she had a responsible job, they lived comfortably. And I couldn't blame her for fighting. I was the one who had turned the children over to her. Like virtually every male I know who has gone through a divorce, I had unthinkingly signed away my rights. At this late date I wanted to change the rules of the game. What judge would seriously consider such a plea?

VI

In a country as large and diverse as ours, there must be millions of happily married couples, fathers and mothers and children living together in an atmosphere of mutual respect and love. Unfortunately, I know very few happy people. In the pressure-cooker world of New York City, there never seems to be enough time to relax and enjoy the simple things I remember from my youth. My mother used to pack a lunch and the whole family would spend a long, hot summer afternoon in the shade along the riverbank, splashing in the cool water, fishing, playing tag. Or we would drive to the top of Cumberland Gap and have lunch, sitting on the ground as my father told us about our ancestors who had made their way from Virginia into Kentucky through the gap and on up the valleys to the flatlands around Boonesboro and Lexington. We did most things together as a family. I am sure we five children had to be a burden for my parents, but we didn't feel we were burdens. We were not bombarded from every side with the disquieting news that our mother was in bondage because she had to take care of us. Nor did we feel our existence was an inconvenience for our father.

I seriously question if some of my friends really love their children. If confronted, they would no doubt insist they loved their offspring; their children give meaning to their lives. But to report that nothing was going wrong somehow meant the parent wasn't really involved. I never heard a simple tale of a child who was muddling through—making it without really making it. Passing but not setting the world on fire; a normal, middle-of-the-road kid who never wanted to go to Harvard anyway. Since I was only a weekend father, I wasn't involved in the day-to-day life of my children. I didn't really understand that living with children is a routine affair, not the hothouse kind of relationship I had with my two. So when my friends discussed their children, they mentioned only the high and low points, the time the son was a sports hero or the daughter scored near the bottom on her S.A.T.'s. I had the impression that their children were merely ego extensions, not independent identities with independent needs and desires. Listening to my friends talk about their children, I could only assume that child care was, at best, unpleasant, if not downright boring.

Few of my friends are still married to their first choice of a mate. Possibly because I am divorced, I move in social circles consisting of people like myself. The current figures on the spiraling divorce rate, however, would indicate that my friends and I are not really exceptional. Divorce has replaced psychoanalysis as the fashionable topic of conversation. When I first moved to New York after World War II, the people I knew who were married used their marriage as the battlefield where they played out the psychodrama of their lives. Everyone was convinced their particular "shrink" was superior to the doctor who listened to the friend's problems. Names of doctors were exchanged with the same casualness as passing on the title of a book one had just read. Today, we pass on the name of the lawyer who got us a better divorce settlement than our friend was able to get. Many of my friends' marriages ended in a divorce court long before it occurred to me that my own would one day go the same route. Few of these friends, however, gave me any usable advice as far as my relationship with my children was concerned.

"Don't ever abandon those children," an older friend did tell me one Sunday night after I had put my two on the train for Westchester County. "You'll regret it the rest of your life."

"Are you speaking from experience?" I asked. I knew he had been divorced a number of years before, but he had never mentioned children.

"I had two. A boy and a girl. Their mother moved back to Chicago when we were divorced, and within a year neither of them would have anything to do with me. She turned them against me . . . women do that, sometimes on purpose, sometimes because they can't help taking their hatred out on the children. Anyway, it happens. Later she married again and her new husband adopted my children, giving them his name. Regardless of what, it was my fault too that the children turned against me. I just walked away and didn't make any effort to keep in touch with the kids. The reason I'm telling you this is that last week I was in Chicago on business and I saw a newspaper article about my son. He's a promising young lawyer who is becoming involved in politics. He's my son and I don't even know him. And he doesn't know me."

"Did you call him? Let him know you were in town?"

"No. That's all water over the dam. But don't make the mistake I did. Don't abandon them. Let them know you care."

"You know I love my children."

"I know, but that isn't important. Make damn sure they know it."

I took my friend's advice. I never faded into the background of my children's lives, the way so many of my friends have done. It wasn't until I started telling people I was seriously working on gaining custody of Preston that I realized how far into the background most of them had drifted. Not a single one of my male friends thought I should even make the effort.

"Look, he has only four more years, then he'll be leaving home for college and well rid of the both of you," Ben told me. "It's only growing pains. Every boy wants to run away from home. I did at that age, only I didn't have a dad to run to, so I stuck it out. I'm no worse for it."

"If your son asked to move in with you, what would you tell him?"

"I'd have to be honest with the kid. I couldn't cope with him here in the city. I've just bought him a car. He's got everything he ever dreamed of having. He wouldn't want to live with me anyway. We don't get along that well."

Another friend was much more candid. "I don't think you know what you're getting yourself into," he warned me. Then he told me something I hadn't known before. A couple of years earlier he had reluctantly agreed to take his fifteen-year-old son off his ex-wife's hands—she had remarried and the boy didn't get along with the new husband. So Sid picked up the boy and brought him into the city. Their life together had been a disaster. Unfortunately, children understand more than we think they do. The boy knew he was being dumped on his father and that essentially his father considered it an inconvenience to have him around.

"After two months the kid ran away and was picked up in Florida on a drug charge," Sid told me.

"Why did he run away?"

"It just didn't work out, our living together. He wouldn't do anything I told him to do. He would leave the apartment and I thought he was going to school, but he spent his days roaming around the city. I don't know where he got the money for drugs, but I knew he was on something. I stocked the refrigerator, but he never fixed himself anything to eat."

"You didn't fix him dinner?"

"You know what kind of a schedule I have. I can't get home in time to cook dinner. I provided food; he just couldn't be bothered fixing something for himself. One morning I got up and he hadn't come home the night before. A week later I got a call from Florida. I pulled some strings and got him out, but not before he was gang-raped in his cell. What a goddamn mess."

"Where's the boy now?"

"In Nevada. His mother has an uncle who owns a ranch and the kid is working for him. Seriously, think twice before you bring the boy in. Having a teen-age kid living with you in the city is just one big pain in the neck."

There were as many reasons for not taking their children

as there were men I talked to. One had recently remarried and didn't think it would be fair to his new wife to stick her with children from an earlier marriage. Another insisted it was a woman's place to care for children.

Talking with my male friends made me feel a little grubby. All of them had an excuse that eased their minds; they didn't feel guilty for not wanting their children. What made me feel uncomfortable was that a few months earlier I probably would have had a similar excuse. As much as I resented alimony and child-support payments, it would never have occurred to me to lift a finger to gain custody of the children. My friends and I didn't need the added inconvenience of caring for our children.

The divorced women I know look down the long road quite differently than the male. In the first place, they automatically accept their responsibility to care for the young —and if possible, to exclude the male from any influence in the growing up of the children. Jane, a woman I have known for a long time, urged me not to go through with any attempt to gain custody. "You'll not be able to pull it off and the boy will be worse off than if he'd stuck it out with his mother."

Jane's son was a year younger than Preston, her daughter a couple of years older. She has been divorced for five years. Her ex-husband has, for all practical purposes, dropped out of his children's lives. He married his young secretary and the two of them took off for the West Coast. It seems he is often between jobs and the alimony checks are, at best, irregular. In the beginning the children flew out for Christmas and for a month in the summer. But when his new wife gave birth to a son, the relationship between the older children and the new wife became so strained that they stopped going out to see him. They never mention their father when I am around.

Jane's son is often in some sort of trouble. Jane caught him smoking grass in his bedroom when he was only twelve. The headmaster of the school he attended informed Jane the boy would not be welcome back in the fall and suggested she make other arrangements. He beat up on a younger boy in the playground in the park, and the mother of the child called the police. There was always something going wrong.

"Have you ever thought about sending the boy out to live with his father?" I suggested one day when Jane was telling me about her latest crisis.

"In the first place, the bastard would just put the kid on the next plane back East. He couldn't be bothered. He's got a new family to worry about." After a pause she added, "Anyway, I would never give up the boy. He's difficult to deal with, but he's mine. I'll cope with him, thank you."

Another friend often complained that her ex-husband never took the children off her hands. "God, I only wish he would take them for a month, the way you take yours. A whole month without having to rush home from the office every night to fix dinner. A Saturday morning when I wouldn't have to get up because they were sleeping over with their father. He couldn't care less about his children. He's too busy being 'Mr. Stud' around town to spend time with his kids."

"You have a career. You need your freedom. Why don't you suggest that he take the children?"

"He wouldn't take them. And I wouldn't let them go. They are my children. Do you know what my reputation would be around town if I willingly gave up my children? You must be joking."

My women friends are caught on the other horn of the dilemma. Although some of them might, secretly, want to be free of the responsibility of caring for their children, they could never admit it. They have been as conditioned as their ex-husbands to believe only women care for children. Regardless of how tied down they feel, regardless of how much they resent having to cook and clean and do the laundry on top of trying to make it in the business world, they could never turn their children over to their ex-husbands. To give up the children would be to admit being a total failure as a woman. A man can walk away from his children and society will accept his actions. He isn't considered an untouchable; it's done every day. But for a woman to willingly give up her children goes against the social grain of our society. She might as well be wearing the scarlet "A" on her chest. They are as much a victim of the outworn cliché of "mother instinct" as the male, but the women I know are not prepared to give in. They are still reacting as a lioness might when her cub is endangered—they will fight to the death to prevent anyone from taking their children from them.

"Do you believe in the idea of the mother instinct?" I asked a friend who has three grown children and is beyond having to defend her brood.

"A lot of bunk," she answered. "You know, when my first boy was born, I sat up in the hospital bed and the nurse put the tiny thing in my arms. And I waited for that good ole mother instinct to strike. All I felt was panic. That tiny child was my sole responsibility and I didn't have the vaguest idea of how to care for him. But

I learned. It's a learning process, for heaven's sake. It's not something you're born with. You learn to listen to their cries and know when they are hungry, or wet, or just mad."

"Could a man learn the same thing?" I asked.

"Of course. But show me one who wants to learn. We're stuck with the children, so we learn whether or not we want to. We've no choice."

"Would you ever have considered letting your husband have the children when you were divorced?"

"I would never have let him have them. Never in a thousand years. They were my children. Anyway, he was a drunk and couldn't have cared less about his three. I've raised them all by myself."

(It wasn't until I started talking with my women friends about custody that I realized that virtually every one of them mentioned at some point that the reason for the divorce was that her husband was a drunk. I've known some of these ex-husbands, and they either have sobered up or were being falsely accused. I wonder if it hasn't become the fashionable excuse for the breakup of a marriage. It is certainly a more acceptable explanation than having to admit that the passion was gone and that there wasn't a solid enough base of friendship to hold the marriage together.)

Without exception, my women friends felt it would be a terrible mistake for me to gain custody of Preston. The child would be much worse off with me than with his mother. My own mother echoed their opinion.

"What do you know about taking care of a teen-age boy?" she asked the night I talked to her about Preston's plans. Then she laughed. The idea that I might end up caring for my son struck her as funny. "You'd better go out and buy yourself a cookbook and start practicing, just in case."

"I have a cookbook and I've been cooking for the children on weekends for four years. And I cook for myself."

"Grilling a steak isn't cooking. The boy can't live on hamburgers and steaks day after day. Do you have a washing machine? Is there one in your building?"

"There is, but I never use it. I drop the stuff off at a place around the corner and pick it up on the way home. I can cope with the laundry, for heaven's sake."

"Look, he'll be all right where he is. His mother isn't mean to him. She takes good care of him. He's probably better off where he is."

My mother didn't go so far as to tell me that children need their mothers, or that she thought I was totally incapable of caring for him, but I got her message. Even though she had never been particularly fond of Vanessa, she still thought her grandson would be better off staying in the country.

No one I talked to ever brought up the possibility that it might be in Preston's best interest for him to live with me. There was a tiny minority of two who thought it was a good idea . . . Preston and the psychiatrist.

The first weekend in April was my turn to have the children. Time was running out. September wasn't that far away and I hadn't faced the most difficult problem of all. I had not called my lawyer.

On Saturday night, when Preston and I were talking after Molly had gone to sleep, he seemed troubled.

"When are you going to tell Mom that I'm moving in?" he asked. "Look, Dad, I won't be any problem. I'm old enough so I won't need baby-sitters. You can still go out.

I can do things around the apartment. Take out the garbage, help you. I really won't be a problem."

I felt as though I had been caught in a lie. On one level I had been lying to him, at least in the beginning. And he had sensed my doubts and was, in his own way, calling my bluff. He had been sprawled on the bed, his head resting on his arm. He swung his feet off the bed and sat up. "I am going to move in with you, aren't I, Dad?" Tears were rising in his eyes.

"Yes, Preston. Yes, you are going to move in with me. And I know you won't be any problem. We'll get it all settled soon. Don't worry about it."

On Monday morning I would call the lawyer. I had reached fail-safe; there was no turning back. As much as I dreaded what lay ahead, I knew I had used up all my options.

VII

I left the office an hour before I was to meet Vanessa and took a long walk up Fifth Avenue. It was late April and Central Park was bursting with spring. But my mind wasn't on the plum blossoms. How was I going to tell her that it was best that Preston move in with me? How could I explain that the relationship the boy and I had was so important to him that the doctor felt it was imperative that he live with me? She was his mother; she loved him. Could I make her understand that she hadn't failed in her responsibilities as his mother—that I didn't think I was a better parent? It wasn't a case of better or best. We were just different kinds of people and Preston responded to me differently than he did to his mother. If I could present his case in such a way that she could accept his moving in, the last barrier would have fallen. If I tripped up, there would surely be chaos.

"It could take months, even years, to fight something like this through the courts," my lawyer had warned me when I called.

"I don't have months. I only have weeks."

"We don't have a solid enough case. We really don't."

The only solution Jim could recommend was a meeting with Vanessa. Two intelligent, rational people sitting down to discuss a problem which concerned both of us . . . the welfare of our son. If we put the boy's needs above our own feelings, we could surely work out an arrangement whereby Preston could live with me and still keep an open channel to his mother. It simply had to work. Too much was at stake.

I arrived at the restaurant ten minutes early and took a table where I thought we could talk without being overheard. When I made the appointment to meet her, I had given no clue as to what I wanted to discuss with her. All I had said was that I wanted to talk to her about something regarding the children and that I didn't think we should do it over the phone. It had been more than four years since we spent any time together. We were in touch arranging the children's schedules and vacations. At the end of summer vacations she usually drove in to pick up the kids, but that was the extent of our contact. Had we lived in the same town, we probably would have had more reason to see each other. A number of my friends go by their former wife's apartment to pick up their children. My two commuted by train. They went from one world to the other, and the two worlds were distinct and quite separate.

Some friends have claimed that theirs was a "friendly" divorce—that they get along fine with their ex-wife. I have to take their word for it. For a number of reasons, Vanessa and I had not managed to put our relationship on a "friendly" footing. I knew I had to blunt as much of the bitterness between us as I could if I was to convince her of the wisdom of Preston's desire to live with me.

When she arrived I ordered her a drink and we chatted briefly about our careers, some needed repairs on the house, the soaring cost of living. I had the sinking feeling she expected me to discuss the possibility of increasing my support payments. There was nothing for me to do but plunge in and, sink or swim, let her know why I had invited her to dinner.

"Preston wants to move in with me in September," I told her. "I've taken him to see a psychiatrist, who feels that it is absolutely necessary that the boy live with me."

A silence as suffocating as a Los Angeles smog settled over the table. I watched her back stiffen, the expression on her face freeze in a noncommittal smile. She began asking questions. When had Preston asked to move in? How was I going to care for him?—I traveled a lot and he couldn't be left alone. What about school? I answered as accurately as I could, always aware that she had to be suffering almost unbearable pain. I could not share with her my own doubts of my ability to care for the boy. I did try to make her understand I did not think I was a better parent than she was; we were different people, with different emotional reactions to life. I am more easygoing than she, and Preston needed the kind of emotional exchange life with me would provide. I knew her financial position and offered to continue sending her Preston's support payments after he moved in. For Molly's sake, I didn't want any added pressures that could be avoided.

"I think it is a terrible mistake," she said finally and my heart skipped a beat. "A terrible mistake," she repeated.

"You've turned my son against me, against his mother. What a terrible thing to do to Preston, to me."

If I told her of my sleepless nights, worrying about whether I was capable of taking care of him; if I told her that it was Preston's wish and his wish alone, she would have been even more hurt. Before meeting Vanessa, I had tried to think of how I would feel if confronted with the same kind of information, how deeply wounded I would be. I didn't want to hurt her and if thinking I had turned the boy against her lessened the pain, then I would let her think it.

She sighed and crushed out her cigarette and lit another. Smoke hung like a gray mist above her head. "If Preston doesn't want to live with me, I won't do anything to stop his moving in. I do want another professional opinion and I want a chance to talk him out of it."

I felt my body go limp. I had been so tense that when I relaxed, I sagged in my chair. Vanessa had risen above her own hurt to the point where she considered Preston's needs ahead of her own feelings. There was nothing more to say. Neither of us was hungry. We finished our drinks and went our separate ways.

Two days later I learned she had agreed to let Preston move in. For the next few weeks I was mentally and emotionally numb. Like Dorothy, I had been sucked up in the funnel of a tornado and deposited in Oz. Preston was moving into the city in September and I was going to have to make radical adjustments in my life style. Financially, I would be pushed to the wall. My obligations to the house in the country were to remain the same, but I had added school fees as well as the cost of feeding and clothing a rapidly growing boy. We would have to share the same bedroom—I certainly couldn't afford to move at this point. I was going to need all the luck I could get to pull this off.

Molly's reaction to the news was one of hurt and anger and bewilderment. In my emotional fog I was only vaguely aware that she had become remote, and for her, very quiet, during the weekends she was with me following the final decision. Preston and I had started making plans that did not include her. The tight threesome which had done everything together for years had suddenly become a twosome, with Molly tagging along. It was late May before I realized that she was physically separating herself from Preston and me, lagging behind us when we walked down the street. She let Preston dominate the conversation at dinner and often watched television so intently that she either pretended not to or actually did not hear us talking to her. Thoughtlessly, we had cut her out. It wasn't Preston's fault. He was so full of himself, so relieved the years of waiting were finally coming to an end that he could think of nothing else. But I should have been thinking of Molly and the effect Preston's move would have on her. She dearly loved her brother, and he, like her father, was going to abandon her.

I had been so preoccupied that I also had given no further thought to our summer vacation. In early June, when I was having a chat with Molly before she went to bed, she put her arms around my neck and hugged me very tightly. When she relaxed, she leaned back and looked me directly in the eye. "Dad, does Preston's moving in mean we can't go to Yugoslavia?"

Not to go would mean that because of Preston, Molly was being denied something she had counted on. To go would be financially ruinous. But it would be better to struggle with overdue bills than to let Molly think I was more concerned for her brother than I was about her. The news of his desire to live with me had been a shattering experience for her. She couldn't understand the emotional tension that had settled over her life. We would have to go to Yugoslavia and worry later about how to manage financially.

I had made airline reservations before Vanessa agreed to let Preston move in and I hadn't bothered canceling them. "We leave on the first of August," I told Molly. "We're going to have a grand vacation. Don't worry." She kissed me again and crawled under the covers. "I love you, Daddy," she muttered into her pillow.

Yugoslavia was an inspired choice for a vacation which represented the end of a kind of innocence for the children. For a month, we were suspended in time. New York was thousands of miles away and the problems and doubts of the past few months had been left behind, not to concern us until we returned.

We lived from day to day with a joyous intensity the three of us had not experienced before. The usual and expected bickering between the children had evaporated even before we left for the airport in New York, where we were greeted with the news that our flight was going to be delayed for at least two hours. The schedule was tight; we were to change planes in Amsterdam for the flight to Belgrade with only an hour's layover. So we would miss our flight. The children weren't concerned, as I had expected them to be. They played backgammon in the bar while I fortified myself for the takeoff of the lumbering 747 (takeoffs in the huge airbuses are much worse than in the conventional planes . . . it's like sitting in a hotel lobby and praying all that weight can defy the laws of gravity). When we finally landed in Amsterdam, nearly three hours late, I found that the punctual Dutch had taken care of everything. There were two other passengers on our flight with a connection to Belgrade, and the KLM agents had talked Yugoslav Airlines into holding its departure for five late arrivals.

Late in the afternoon we landed in the kind of heat I associate with the tropics. Athens and Madrid had been hot in August, but Belgrade was sweltering in a record-breaking heat wave. After one of the wildest taxi rides I have ever experienced—the driver thought nothing of going up on the sidewalk on the wrong side to pass a slower car—we were deposited at the Metropol, a gracious but non-air-conditioned hotel in the middle of the city. The children were quite unconcerned. Once we were shown to our rooms, Preston started figuring out how to convert dinars into dollars, Molly hung up her dresses and I soaked in a cold bath.

We had dinner in the hotel's terrace restaurant, then took a walk along the tree-lined boulevard in front of the hotel. The two of them walked ahead of me, peering into shop windows, laughing at jokes I couldn't overhear. They were happy, relaxed, totally involved in the moment. I was the third wheel, catching up with them when they stopped to look at camera equipment in a window, or waiting at a crosswalk for the light to change. It was as though they had decided to make this vacation somehow memorable, something they could remember long after the agony of September was forgotten. And when I should have been feeling happy and relaxed along with them, I began to feel a kind of sadness. This wasn't the last vacation the three of us would have together; Preston's move into the city didn't mean Molly was going to be cut out of our lives. But his move was a rite of passage, the end of one chapter of our lives and the beginning of a new, and unknown, future.

After five days in the sizzling heat of Belgrade—sadly enough, one of the dullest capitals in Europe; the city has been leveled by wars so many times that only ten buildings are more than two hundred years old—we picked up our rented car and headed south. When I told the bartender in our hotel that we were going to drive throughout the country, he warned me to be very careful on the highways. The Turks, he told me, drive through Yugoslavia on their way home from jobs in Germany and they are crazy drivers. They drive straight through because they can't afford hotels, and their fatigue, coupled with excessive drinking, according to the knowledgeable barkeep, made the highways deathtraps. We were only an hour out of Belgrade when we came across the first accident. But it wasn't a car with Turkish plates. A German car had rammed head-on into a Yugoslav truck loaded with cattle on the way to market. A messy, noisy scene. During the month, we saw a number of accidents along the highways, and in each case a German car was involved. I learned to fear the German drivers much more than the Turkish. As we had noticed in Spain the year before, German drivers are suicidal, their egos requiring them to dominate the highways even if it means passing on curves.

Our first stop south of Belgrade was Sarajevo. We were once again traveling without reservations, but the desk clerk at the Metropol had called ahead and booked us into the Europa. The spirit of Rebecca West still haunts the corridors of the old hotel. Our room overlooked an outdoor café where a rock-'n'-roll band played American music, the dance floor jammed with jean-clad youths gyrating to the same music teen-agers in Kansas City or Dallas were dancing to. In the mornings we were awakened by the Moslem call to prayers from the minaret of the mosque just beyond the café. The past and the present overlapped like the patterns of the handmade Bosnian rugs displayed in shops in the Turkish sector of the town. Molly posed for Preston, standing in the footprints embedded in cement on the corner where the young anarchist Princip fired the shots at Archduke Ferdinand which ignited World War I. Sarajevo is a city of extreme contrasts—modern factories belching soot which settles on the tile roofs of houses built by Turkish conquerors in the sixteenth century.

The highway leading from Sarajevo to Mostar snakes through some of the most spectacular mountains I have ever seen. These forbidding cliffs protected the Tito Partisans during World War II. I told the children what I knew of the heroic struggle of the Partisans who had managed to pin down forty German divisions during the war, causing Hitler to make the fatal decision to delay his attack on Russia. While we were driving through Yugoslavia I realized how very little I knew about the country's history. For centuries the land had been the doormat of Europe, with wave after wave of conquerors sweeping across the land. One man we met had been a citizen of three nations in his lifetime without leaving his native village.

It wasn't just that the children were a year older than when we had driven through Spain; they were more intense, more determined to enjoy themselves. They seemed to be absorbing each day through their pores. Their laughter was easy and light. They sat next to each other in restaurants, when before, Preston would have slid into the seat beside me, with Molly sitting across from us. In Mostar we found rooms in a hotel on the bank of the Neretva. Just down the river was the historic stone bridge, the oldest arched bridge extant in Europe, which had been built by the Turkish bey in 1556. We had lunch at a restaurant on the river's edge, Preston constantly snapping pictures of Molly and the bridge. Mostar is still a Turkish village, a part of the past. If it weren't for the traffic jams in the town square, it would be easy to go back in one's mind to the town Andric wrote about in *The Bridge on the Drina*. There are more than forty mosques, and the call to prayers echoes up and down the valley.

Out last night in Mostar was a Sunday. The dining room of our hotel was mobbed by local residents who could afford to dine out one night a week. When we finally were shown to a table, the captain asked if he could also seat a young German woman who was traveling alone. She was a schoolteacher who spoke excellent English, and she spent most of dinner telling the children how bad American schools were. She had visited America and thought American students were lazy. It was quite obvious she had as little use for our homeland as I had for hers. Over coffee, she asked me what I thought about the resignation of our President. I had not seen an English-language newspaper since we left Belgrade. German is the second language in Yugoslavia and the kiosks in the less traveled parts of the country didn't bother with the Paris *Herald*. I knew nothing of Nixon's resignation.

"Several days ago. He's now swimming in the Pacific,"

she told us, complete with breaststrokes sweeping over the coffee cups. There was undisguised glee in her voice.

We arrived in Dubrovnik just after lunch the next day. Despite dire warnings from hotel clerks along the way that we would have to sleep on the beach because Dubrovnik hotels were completely booked, we found the lovely Argentine Hotel, built on a cliff overlooking the old walled city, could put us up for five nights. Preston and Molly set out to find a kiosk and an English-language newspaper while I unpacked. They came back empty-handed; I would have to wait another day to find out what had prompted Nixon to take his swim in the Pacific. We decided to take a swim in the Adriatic, to hell with overambitious men and corrupt governments and all the rest of it.

Dubrovnik is one of the few tourist attractions which look better in reality than in the colorful posters on travel agents' walls. After a swim in the morning we dressed and walked down to a restaurant inside the walled city with a spectacular view of the old harbor. Service was slow, but the food excellent and we had nothing more important to do than sit and watch the fishing boats bobbing on their anchors and the sea gulls diving for food. Later we wandered the cobblestone streets worn smooth by generations of fiercely proud Slavs who had managed to keep the tiny city/state neutral during most of Yugoslavia's turbulent history.

The cloudless sky, the soft breeze off the sea, drained us of any sense of urgency. Our vacation was more than half over, but there was still time to sit by the sea, to walk ancient streets, to laugh at meaningless jokes, to read about the people and places we had visited. After five days we drove on down the coast to Sveti Stefan, near the Albanian border, for four more days of sitting in the sun. In the evenings we listened to a small dance band in the rooftop café and watched the moon come up from behind the mountains of Albania.

By the time we reached the island of Hvar, the children had had enough of beaches and historic ruins and hilltop monasteries. After breakfast we sat on the balcony of our hotel overlooking the bay and played backgammon or read. The Paris *Herald* arrived on the noon boat, so we walked around the point to the harbor and had lunch at the café along the quay. I lingered over coffee and read the paper while the children roamed around the ancient square, taking pictures and talking with English-speaking tourists. They didn't seem to be bored with the quiet life in the fifteenth-century village. They couldn't have cared less about the history of the ruins of the fort that jut into the pale-blue sky from the top of the hill, or the thirteenth-century arsenal which houses the oldest theater in the Western world.

In four days we must be in Zagreb to catch our plane for home. If only it were possible to grab a moment out of the stream of time and hold it long enough to truly savor the sounds, the smells, the emotions contained in fleeting seconds which slip past into memory before one has time to really experience them. The sun was setting behind the mountain, casting long shadows across the quay. Two chess players at the next table sat like statues, staring at the board before them. In the distance, the tolling of church bells. Inside the café, a radio was playing Serbian folk songs. Preston and Molly were sitting on the edge of the dock watching local women buying fresh vegetables from a boatman from another island. We would have to deal with

New York in four days, but today we were in the fifteenth century. A soft breeze rustled the leaves of the trees along the harbor.

Why do we have to go home? No one had mentioned Preston's move during the entire vacation. It was as though by not talking about the future, the future didn't exist. There was only now, today, the sound of the waves slapping against the dock. The future did exist and the last day we spent in Hvar seemed to me so very, very short.

We had lingered too long on the Dalmatian coast. It was a real push to arrive in Zagreb in time to turn in the car and do some last-minute shopping. On our last night in Yugoslavia the children used up the last of our dinars in the slot machines in the casino at the Esplanade Hotel. They went to bed early, exhausted from a month none of us would soon forget.

I lingered at the bar for a nightcap. When I told the bartender we had driven throughout the country for a month, he was most concerned. And I heard the same story I had heard in Belgrade about the terrible Turks.

"All the accidents we saw involved crazy German drivers," I told him. His eyes shifted to the other end of the bar, where two German businessmen were obviously listening to our conversation. I didn't wish to spoil my last night by having to deal with any more Germans, so I paid my check and went up to bed.

The Esplanade Hotel is located next to the train station. There seemed to be a great deal of confusion around the station the next morning when we headed out to the airport, but the taxi driver didn't speak English and it wasn't until I read the New York *Times* the next day that I learned there had been a serious accident in the Zagreb station the day we left. Scores of Yugoslav workers on their way to their jobs in Germany had been killed. The account of the accident went into lengthy detail about why more than five hundred workers were on the train headed for Germany. According to the *Times*, the men were afraid to drive to Germany because of the terrible Turks on the highway. There was no mention of the fact that most of the people on the train were peasants and could not have afforded to own a car.

"At least you drink in the same bars as the *Times* reporter," Preston observed.

Preston and Molly went to Westchester County the day after we returned. In one week I would rent a car and drive up to collect Preston's belongings. Molly's face was drawn when I kissed her goodbye. The dream had ended. We were back in the twentieth century.

VIII

Nothing much had changed in the living room since I moved out of the house nearly five years before. There was a new bookcase against one wall, but the two overstuffed chairs still flanked the fireplace, and the sofa, the sideboard, the highboy and the glass cabinet were in the same places they had been put when we first moved into the house. The room hadn't really changed, but I had, and I felt a stranger in a house that had been, for years, both my castle and my prison. The room seemed smaller than I remembered, less hospitable. The aroma of my pipe tobacco had long been aired from the house; the new smell was alien. It was like running into someone on the street who, for whatever reason, you no longer considered a friend. He looks different, only he hasn't changed; you just look at him with different eyes. It was uncomfortable to stand in a room that had once been "our" home and know that I was an outsider.

Preston had been a small boy when I last saw him in this room. It was a young adult who was lugging box after box out to the car; his lifelong collection of banners and pictures and books and microscopes and rocks and piggy banks and baseball gloves. Molly helped us load the car, and when we finished, she began to cry. She hugged me tightly, almost desperately, then followed the car to the end of the driveway, still waving as we disappeared over the top of the hill.

For several miles, neither of us spoke. I was deeply troubled about Molly. There was something wrenching in picking up the belongings of one of my children and leaving the other one in a house that would never again be quite the same. As we drove along the highway I wished I hadn't gone back into the house. Too many memories, some mellow, some painful, had been dredged to the surface—memories I had put behind me as I rebuilt my life in the city. The long evenings sitting in front of the fireplace watching the flames darting over the logs, the room full of the sounds of a Beethoven quartet; the quiet dinner parties with friends who had driven up from the city; the large Christmas trees with the funny-looking Santa ornament I had bought for Preston's first Christmas and the white birds I had added on Molly's first holiday. The emotional investment I had put into the house, into my life with my children, now seemed hollow, the memories elusive, almost dreamlike.

"May I turn on the radio?" Preston asked, his voice tight.

He found a station he knew, and the sounds of electric guitars and squeaky male voices shattered the stillness. It was a warm, still-summer, September day. The traffic was light and we were making good time. Soon we would be back in the city and a new life would begin for both of us. As we approached the George Washington Bridge, Preston sighed. He leaned back against the seat and locked his fingers together behind his head.

"It wasn't as bad as I thought it would be," he said, almost to himself. "Where are we going to put all of my stuff?"

"I haven't the faintest idea. I can't think beyond getting all the boxes up to the apartment. I didn't know you had so much. Do you ever throw anything away?"

"Do you? Your apartment is full of junk."

"Our apartment," I reminded him.

"Yeah. Our apartment."

I left Preston to lug the boxes while I returned the car to the rental agency. When I got back, he was sprawled on the sofa listening to the radio. The living-room floor was knee-deep with the odds and ends of his life. I had been thinking in terms of his clothes and had emptied out a closet and a couple of drawers in my large dresser. I had also purchased a desk for the bedroom. It had never occurred to me that I would have to find storage space for a coconut from Puerto Rico, bullfight posters from Spain, several boxes of spy mysteries, a chemistry set, stacks of boxed games and ship models.

It had also not occurred to me that I should have stopped by the supermarket and stocked the refrigerator. There was nothing for dinner, so we went up the street to a restaurant, leaving the chaos to be dealt with later. Both of us were tired and emotionally drained. Neither said much. Preston devoured a large steak, a baked potato and a salad. What did he eat every night? Certainly he had not been existing on expensive steaks, but what did he like? I had never asked him what sort of food his mother had served night after night, week after week. Unfortunately I couldn't call her to find out. It would have been grossly unfair to her. All I could do was make my own mistakes and depend on Preston to give me tips on what he liked and didn't like . . . within the limited range of my cooking abilities. I was quite certain he didn't expect the kind of varied menus we enjoyed while on vacation.

After dinner we watched television and he turned in early. We were past the age when I kissed him good night. He waved to me from the bedroom door.

"Sleep well," I told him.

"Don't worry, I will. Thanks, Dad."

"For what?"

"Letting me move in with you. I love you."

"Good night, son."

After he went to bed I watched the late news, then tried to write in my journal, but too much had happened during the day, feelings that were still ill-defined and difficult to pin down. Surrounded by the clutter, I turned on the radio and tried to concentrate on a book. At two I gave up and went into the bedroom. My son was sleeping soundly, his arms curled around the pillow, his hair falling across his eyes. I would have to find a barber for him. He also needed new clothes. He had grown over the summer and most of his clothes were too small.

My last thoughts before dropping off to sleep were of Molly. In my mind's eye I could still see her standing at the end of the driveway, waving to us as we drove up over the hill and headed toward the city and our new life together. What effect would Preston's move have on her? What had the two of us done to her, leaving her in the country, cutting her out of our life together in the city? "Deal with one thing at a time," I had been told. The one thing I had to deal with right now was Preston, sleeping soundly in the bed across the room, his breathing even and untroubled. One thing at a time.

The next day we made an attempt to organize some of his possessions, to stash some of them away in a closet, to get his clothes hung up or put into drawers. During the afternoon we took a long walk along Riverside Drive, snooping on the people whose life style includes living on houseboats moored at the Seventy-ninth Street marina. On the way back to the apartment I shopped for some vegetables and a chicken. I would fix what, for lack of a better name, we called "hunter's chicken" . . . nothing more than a chicken stew cooked in a cup of white wine.

After browning the chicken and preparing the vegetables, we returned to the mess in the middle of the living-room floor. One of the first things I was going to have to do was put up more bookcases in the bedroom. When I suggested that some of the litter could be tossed out, Preston became indignant. "I've already thrown away all of the things I don't want," he insisted. We were stuck with finding some way to store what he had not thrown away. We certainly couldn't survive in an apartment with the living-room rug buried under layers of Preston's prized possessions. In our concentration on pulling the apartment back together, I totally forgot about the chicken—until I became aware of a strong burning smell. Dinner was beyond salvage. We retreated to the pizza shop at the corner.

We were crossing the street on our way back to the apartment when Preston asked about his lunch for tomorrow. "Your school has a lunchroom," I reminded him.

"You haven't been in school for a long time. You've forgotten school lunchrooms are the pits. I take my lunch to school."

"What do you have for lunch? What did your mother fix for you?"

"Sandwiches."

"Made of what?"

"Whatever. And fruit."

"Sandwiches made of 'whatever' and fruit. You're a big help. You're sure you don't want to eat in the lunchroom?"

"Positive."

We headed for the deli for a ham and cheese on a roll and stopped by the fruit store for apples and oranges. Why, I wanted to ask over and over again, couldn't he buy himself a hot lunch at school? I really hadn't counted on fixing his lunch every morning.

He set the alarm for six-thirty the next morning. While he was taking a shower I scrambled eggs and prepared toast and juice. At seven-fifteen I pulled on some clothes and went with him to the corner where the bus company told us he would be picked up at seven twenty-six. The bus was late and I was afraid that we had not read the instructions correctly. When it finally arrived, Preston climbed aboard, waved goodbye and headed off for his first day in high school. As the bus pulled away, I remembered the first day he had waited at the end of the driveway for the bus that was to take him to his first day of school in the country. Had it really been eight years? I had watched from the bedroom window as he climbed up the steps, his Flintstone lunch box clutched under his arm. Off alone for the first time in his life. Now, once again, off alone for the first day in a new school, his lunch in a brown paper bag. What had happened to those eight years? They had gone so fast, so much had happened to all of us.

I piled the dirty dishes in the sink and went back to bed. Six-thirty was an uncivilized hour to get up in the morning. Preston was used to it, and I had been used to it when I had to leave the house at eight to catch my train to the city. But that was all in the past. If I got up at nine, I could easily make the office by ten. I reset the clock and dropped off to sleep.

The laundry hamper was spilling dirty shorts onto the closet floor. On the way to work I dropped off the bags with the little man who ran the laundromat around the corner. It would be ready when I returned home in the evening. The office was almost like a haven in the storm. No piles of books on the floor, no boxes of rocks from various beaches around the world. Since I had been so distracted for the past week, my desk was piled with work that had to be finished. It was almost fun to dig into the stacks of reports that had to be read, to return the phone calls I had put off. In midafternoon a friend called and suggested that we meet for a drink after work. I accepted without thinking. We often stopped at a bar nearby for a couple before heading home. It was nearly five-thirty before I realized I couldn't have drinks with my friend. I had to dash home, stopping on the way to buy something for dinner, as well as tomorrow's lunch. When I called my friend, he laughed. "I warned you," he reminded me. "You should have left well enough alone. You're going to have to get married so there'll be someone around to care for the kid."

"Not bloody likely. I'll have to learn to manage."

Dinner consisted of an overdone steak, rice and a salad. Preston had been given homework on the first day of school, and after dinner he went into the bedroom and closed the door. The routine of our life together had begun. He had signed up for the fencing team rather than take gym, so he wouldn't get home until nearly six-thirty every night. I would have to somehow manage to have dinner ready not later than seven. At seven-thirty he would start his homework and I would end up in the closet of a kitchen cleaning up. There wasn't enough space to let dishes accumulate for more than one day.

The next morning Preston came into the living room while I was preparing his breakfast. He was wrapped in a towel. "I haven't any clean underwear," he informed me. "Or socks."

I had forgotten to pick up the laundry on the way home. I didn't realize that when he unpacked his clothes, most of his things had been dumped into the laundry hamper. There was nothing I could do. He would have to go to school wearing the same underwear he had worn the day before. He muttered something as he went back into the bedroom about not liking to have to wear dirty shorts and socks. I agreed with him, but there wasn't time for me to go to the laundromat if he was to catch his bus.

After he left I dressed and went over to pick up the laundry and was unpleasantly surprised to learn that it was a Jewish holiday. The place had closed at sundown the day before and would not reopen for two days. Two more days of wearing the same shorts and socks unless I bought new ones. But I didn't know what size to buy. I had never bought him underwear before.

"He's fourteen and about five feet tall," I told the saleslady. "And thin. He's thin."

"Why don't you call your wife, she'll know what size he needs."

"I'm not married and he lives with me."

"Look in the back of what he's wearing. It'll tell you what size he needs. It's on the label."

"I wear shorts and know the size is on the label. But they're all in the laundry. I forgot to pick up the laundry and it's a Jewish holiday and . . ."

The saleslady gave me a withering look. "Here. Take a package of three in size 32–34. That'll probably fit, but don't buy any more until you know what size he wears. I'll give you some stretch socks. He's only fourteen and lives with you?"

"Yes," I muttered, handing her the money. I longed to flee the store before she learned more about my ineptness. Her attitude made me feel decidedly uncomfortable.

By Friday I realized that shopping for dinner on the way home was, at the very least, inefficient and nerve-wracking. I couldn't plan what to buy after I got to the subway. Inevitably, I bought something I already had, or didn't buy something I needed. And I consistently forgot to buy the "whatever" for his lunch and would have to go out again.

So, on Friday night, while Preston was watching television, I plowed through a cookbook trying to find recipes that didn't take hours to prepare. I put two columns on a legal pad, one column with the day of the week and the proposed menu. Monday—pork chops. Tuesday—chicken. Wednesday—chili. And so on. In the other column I listed all of the ingredients. One can cream of mushroom soup, can of tomato soup, rice, thyme, basil, bay leaves, and on and on. I also listed vegetables that seemed easy to prepare. One pound of green beans, eggplant, fresh tomatoes, lettuce. The completed list was most impressive. I was quite pleased with myself.

On my way to the supermarket I stopped by the hardware store for a grocery cart. I had never needed one before. I was now a full-fledged houseperson and for the first time found myself braving the crowds pushing their carts through the aisles on Saturday morning. No one was smiling. There was an air of barely contained hostility, everyone determined to get the whole thing over with as soon as possible. Being a novice to the weekly ritual of buying a week's food supply, I had not developed the necessary protective skills one must have to survive the experience without bruised ankles and frayed temper. Seemingly gentle, educated people fall victim to the mob instinct the moment they get their hands on a shopping cart.

My own cart was spilling over by the time I got to the check-out counter. I had managed to find everything on the list, along with a large number of other cans and cartons that caught my eye. Tomato sauce was on sale, and some of the recipes called for tomato sauce, so I bought six cans. Lima beans were also on sale. Three cans for a dollar. Paper napkins on sale. Stock up. Ground beef in three-pound containers. I could always use ground beef. Grapefruits six to a bag. Three pounds of apples for a dollar. Checking out was a nightmare. And the bill staggering. The poor girl who was packing my cart had to unpack and repack and still couldn't cram all I had purchased into my brand-new two-wheeler, so I was stuck with an additional shopping bag. During the two hours I spent in the store, the weather had ceased to be merely threatening. It was pouring. I was soaked to the skin, my grocery bags a sodden mess, by the time I reached the apartment.

While I changed, Preston began unloading the day's haul. An hour later it was painfully apparent that I had suffered a mental blackout while shopping. The cupboards in my closet-sized kitchen had space for less than half of the cans and boxes I had lugged home. The freezing unit in the refrigerator was so small that I had to remove the ice trays to make room for the meat and cartons of frozen vegetables.

"You ought to shop every week, not just once a month," Preston noted as he helped me stack cans of soup and boxes of napkins under the bar in the living room.

"I intend to shop every week, for goodness' sake." My temper was becoming frayed around the edges.

"Then we'd better start having big dinner parties or find a larger apartment."

His point was well made. I had to organize our lives. Set schedules, make realistic shopping lists and stick to them. So far, the week had been one near-disaster after another. A number of boxes with Preston's belongings were still stacked in the corner of the living room. We had overslept Thursday morning and he had rushed out without breakfast to catch his bus. Despite the large number of boxes and suitcases spread around the apartment, we found that Preston had failed to pack his poncho and snow jacket.

I finally gave up trying to find storage space for all the boxes of rice and noodles and dishwashing liquid (also on sale) and took a nap. I slept longer than I had intended. It was time to start preparing dinner when I roused myself from a dreamless sleep. The rain was pounding against the windows, the wind howling up the flue of the fireplace.

In my attempts to organize the kitchen, I had very carefully placed all the meat in the freezer. The lamb chops I had planned for dinner were already hard as a rock. Despite all my lists, my plans, there wasn't anything in the apartment that could be cooked for dinner. Going to a restaurant was out of the question—Preston had no rain gear. I pulled on my raincoat and trudged to the corner for a pizza.

IX

Caring for very young children is a confining and often frustrating experience. It has to be particularly difficult for a woman who has a career and still must juggle the chores of keeping a single-parent household functioning. Divorced mothers are always pitied by their friends. "Poor Grace. Stuck with her two kids. She never has any time for herself, never has any fun." I suspect Grace rather enjoys feeling sorry for herself. She has an acceptable reason to feel bitter toward her ex-husband, who doesn't spend enough time with his children; a reason to resent her insensitive boss's lack of understanding of how difficult her life is; and especially her new boyfriend, who can't comprehend why he has to be out of the house before the children wake up.

I found, however, these same friends who feel sorry for Grace react very differently when it is the male who is caring for children while keeping a career going. My friends didn't feel sorry for me at all. Quite the opposite. They felt sorry for Preston. I was, after all, a grown man. I hadn't been stuck with my son, as Grace was with her two. Instead, I had gotten myself into this mess and if things didn't work out, I could always ship him back up to his mother, with whom, they were convinced, he should be anyway. "It must be tough, just you and your dad," I overheard one woman tell Preston. "Is the kid getting enough to eat?" a solicitous friend asked.

Both Preston and I began to think of ourselves as freaks. We had defied tradition. Two of the pillars supporting the shaky social arrangements which pass for family life in America were under attack. Preston elected to live with his father, and his father somehow made it possible for him to do so. The whole concept of the "mother instinct" was threatened, as well as the myth of the male's total ineptness as far as caring for a child is concerned. "I must say, you are very brave," one friend said rather condescendingly. "How courageous of you," another said Courage has nothing to do with it. Preston lives with me for the simple reason that it is best that he do so. No one seems to understand we aren't being pioneers; we are simply a father and son living together.

The adjustments Preston and I had to make following his move were, on one hand, much easier than I had imagined, and on the other, much more difficult than I had ever expected. The easy side was the physical adjustments, the sorting out of our daily routines. After the first week of near-total madness, I settled down and made plans. If I could manage an office, then surely I could organize our life together. I already knew some of the obvious pitfalls to avoid. I soon found that Preston's tastes were basically very simple. Despite my own mother's warning, he could, if allowed to, exist on hamburgers and French fries. But he also liked chili, beef stew (which I could prepare over the weekend and warm up), pork chops, baked chicken, ham steaks . . . and tons of salads. I'm quite sure fresh vegetables are more nutritional than the frozen kind, but there simply wasn't time to be elaborate. Just in case, I gave him vitamins every morning.

Since the kitchen was pretty much of a joke, I started accumulating gadgets—an electric frying pan, one of those slow cookers—which could be plugged in on what I originally thought of as a bar in the living room. Within a month I had licked the problem of what to serve for dinner. There were no more wild binges in the supermarket; I bought only what was on my list. I remembered to stop by the deli for roast beef or ham or whatever for his lunch, and the fruit store for oranges and apples.

Preventing the apartment from being condemned by the Health Department was not as easy as organizing a fast-food kitchen. I don't think of myself as overly neat; I like things in their proper place, but I'm certainly not compulsively tidy. However, I had lived alone for over four years and was more a creature of habit than I thought. The toothpaste on the left side of the sink—capped—and shaving cream on the right. When I undress, dirty shirts and shorts go into the hamper, pants on a hanger. After the first week I despaired of ever teaching my son to use closets, bookshelves, dirty-clothes hampers, towel racks. It was too late. In a large house, clutter isn't so obvious. In a small apartment, it's chaos. Socks, books, jeans, sweaters, dirty shorts were strewn across the floor. There had to be a compromise. I staked out the living room—no dirty socks and wet sneakers on the rug, no jacket tossed over the back of the sofa, no books on the floor. In exchange, the bedroom would be his domain and I would not—or at least try not to—bug him too much about the pants left where he stepped out of them, or the damp towel on his bed or the dirty shirt draped over the corner of his desk. My only firm demand was that he leave a clear path through the bedroom to the bathroom door. In the back of my mind, I vainly hoped that, by example, he would learn to stash things away. Sons learn many things from their fathers, but being tidy apparently isn't one of them. When things got totally out of hand, I found it easier to pick up than prod. So we found our compromise.

For the first month I rushed home every night to be with him. Although he spent a great chunk of the evenings at his desk, I felt I should be available when he came up for air between assignments. My just being there, I thought, was all that was necessary. But what kind of a life was I going to have? I had given little thought to how much time I had spent out of the apartment before he moved in; the number of nights I had met friends for dinner in midtown, or stopped off for a drink at a friend's apartment, or gone to the theater. Abruptly, I was cut off from my bachelor life. One evening a couple of friends came over for drinks and it was obvious that Preston found our conversation much more interesting than working on his math. He popped in and out of the bedroom like a yo-yo. I didn't want to be cross with him, to forbid him from joining in the conversation, but he did have work to do. I decided not to invite friends in on a school night.

What kind of a life was I going to be able to make for myself? At his age he certainly could spend the evenings alone, but he hadn't moved in to spend the evenings alone. It was my responsibility, not his, to find the middle ground.

I told myself that once he felt secure in his new life, things would be simpler. By the end of the month I found I enjoyed being alone with him. I still saw my friends at lunch; I wasn't totally cut off from my former life. I realized I had been going out as much as I did because there was no reason not to. There was a reason now to stay home. Things were sorting themselves out for me.

I wasn't so sure about Preston. As the weeks went by, he became more and more evasive, especially when I tried to find out how things were going at school. Had he made any new friends? No. Didn't he like the kids at school? "They're all right, I guess." Would he like to invite his friend (his only friend, I gathered) from the country for a weekend? No. How was schoolwork going? OK. How much homework tonight? Too much. And he would change the subject. We talked about an article he had read in *Science News*, or about something we'd seen on the evening news. We talked often about politics. The shock of going from a public school into the elite atmosphere of a prep school had put a number of his ideas into clearer focus. Why should some children have so many privileges when the majority of the children in New York have so few? I couldn't answer his question. The only time he mentioned school was when he described what he had learned from the fencing coach that day. As far as I knew, he was spending his day in the fencing room, learning to thrust and parry.

I honestly didn't know whether he was happy or sad. Other than on our vacations, I had never spent this kind of time with him, not even when he was young and I still lived with his mother. On vacations there was always a lightness, an airy quality, to his moods. He loved making puns, he laughed easily. That side of him was missing now. He seldom smiled, his conversations were serious, almost intense. I sensed something was terribly wrong. Was he sorry he had moved in? What a chilling thought. Maybe he had expected life with me to be more like the time we spent together on vacation. Unfortunately, life isn't one long vacation. He would have to stick it out, make the adjustment to the way things were. I wished he would discuss what was bothering him.

For years I had heard horror stories about children in trouble, but nothing that explained why the child was out of control. A child does not revolt without a reason. And the reason, as far as I could see, is usually a breakdown in communication between parent and child. How do you reach a teen-ager on an emotional level; how do you let a boy know you want to share what is troubling him? I had the sinking feeling I was slipping into the murky area of no real communication between my son and me. I had assumed, wrongly, that things would be fine once I had managed to organize our life. Things were not going well at all. Obviously our situation was different from most of my friends'. I wasn't a divorced woman stuck with my son. Preston had moved in to be physically near me, to be able to say good night to me every night, not on alternate weekends. I had no idea how to break through, to reestablish the warm, open relationship we had had before.

I did understand that Preston had reason enough to feel sad. The move, although smooth on the surface, had to have been a deeply upsetting experience for him. He came back from his first weekend with his mother physically ill and missed school on Monday because of an upset stomach. Later I learned there were two reasons for his illness. The most obvious was, of course, his feeling of disorientation; two weeks before, the house in the country had been his home and now he was a guest. The other, I found, was that he had not managed to finish his history assignment, and his relationship with his history teacher was already off on the wrong foot.

When I had been stalling in the spring, I made a big issue about schools. If I couldn't place him in a good school, he would have to stay where he was. Now he was going to an excellent school, but something was definitely wrong. There was no point asking Preston, I would only get an evasive answer. I had never dealt with the children's teachers before. Once or twice I had attended parent-teacher conferences, but after I moved back to the city, all involvement with the school ended. I didn't even know where to begin. The only thing I could do was start at the top and see what I could find out.

The dean was most interested in seeing me. From the tone of her voice on the telephone, I knew things were even worse than I had feared. She would see me at my earliest convenience.

I was standing at a window waiting for my appointment when the bell rang and the students began wandering from one building to another. And I saw Preston. He was walking across the campus, physically isolated from the other students, his face a mask. He looked so totally alone, almost alien amid the laughing, carefree students around him. How miserable he must be. Because of his love for me, he had turned his back on his earlier life and now he appeared completely out of place, a boy without friends.

Academically, he was in deep trouble. "He doesn't seem to be able to concentrate," I was told. "All his teachers think he is capable of doing the work, but he isn't applying himself. His homework is consistently late and usually incomplete. How much time does he spend on it?" When I told her, she admitted he should be able to keep up if he was spending that much time at his desk. But was he really working or just sitting, his mind floating off into space? I really didn't know. I had never supervised homework before. Should I ask to see the report he was to turn in or check his math assignment? I could handle an English report, but math was hopeless. I don't understand the rudiments of math. A string of equations across a page could just as well be an Arabic love poem as far as my comprehension is concerned. As it developed, it was indeed his math causing the most concern.

Because of his test scores, he had been placed in an honor's class in geometry where he was competing with the brightest math students in the freshman class. But there had been an administrative slip-up. No one had checked the transcript from his previous school. He had not had algebra in the eighth grade. He was in an honor's class in a course a whole year beyond his abilities. No wonder he was drowning in confusion. No wonder he was beginning to think of himself as a failure. His failure in math was affecting all his other courses. Although the school administration had slipped up, the real responsibility was mine. Instead of feeling puffed up that my son was in an honor's class, I should have been aware that he was not yet ready for the course assigned. The admissions director had alerted me that he would have to make up algebra, but I had put it out of my mind. The solution was administratively simple, but difficult for Preston. He was to be moved down a step in geometry—and was to be privately tutored in algebra. For the entire year he would have to play a game of catch up—something I didn't look forward to.

Preston's five weeks of agony could have been avoided had I not shipped him off to school on the bus that first morning, assuming my job was done. There was more to educating children than had ever crossed my mind. I must learn to participate, to become involved so he would feel he could come to me when things got rough. No wonder he had been so evasive when I tried to discuss his school. He was, or I'm sure he thought he was, letting me down. Actually, I was the one at fault; I should have known better.

"Did he tell you he's talked with the school counselor?"

"No." What else? I thought. Had there been no real communication between us? I was beginning to feel on very shaky ground. Without intending to, the dean gave me the impression that had I been a woman, things would not have gotten to this stage. A woman would intuitively have known what was going on.

"I realize it is difficult for a man to raise a boy alone," she said.

"We're just getting started," I found myself answering.

"I'm sure it will work out. The counselor tells me Preston talks a lot about his sister. He misses her a lot."

After some banal exchanges, some promises that I would stay on top of the situation, I left the school and headed back to my office.

Preston and I were in a lifeboat without oars, drifting far out beyond the sight of land. The boy was paying a terrible price for having made a choice between his parents—and I wasn't being very helpful. I was tied up in emotional knots. If I didn't relax, the situation would only get worse. He was sensitive enough to feel my tension, my fear that he might not succeed at school. I was beginning to understand why some parents simply turn their backs and hope for the best. It wasn't in me to turn my back, but I was baffled and more than a little concerned.

X

While serving in Japan during the Korean War, I was fortunate to get to know James A. Michener, a former history teacher who has retained his interest in the education of the young. Among the nuggets of advice I squirreled away was Michener's dictum: "Always invest in yourself. Travel. Get to know the world."

At the time, I had no idea that I would follow his advice so closely. After the first trip to Europe with the children, I was determined that they should get to know as much of the world as I could manage while they were still young. A wiser, or at least a different, man would have thought more about the saving for college, all the other things prudent fathers are supposed to do. I have never been a prudent man. I hope I never will be and that what the children lack in worldly goods has been made up for in worldly knowledge.

Quite unexpectedly, their knowledge was broadened by what can only be called a bonus trip to Paris two months after Preston's move to the city. In early November I was told I had to attend an international conference in Paris over the Thanksgiving holiday. I was upset by the request. Plans had already been made. Molly was to spend the long weekend in the city with Preston and me. Their mother had accepted an invitation to visit friends. I simply could not screw up everyone's plans. Regardless of the effect on my career, I felt I had to refuse to go. The solution was suggested by my boss: Take the children along.

To take them meant, obviously, that they would have to miss two and a half days of school. For Molly, that wasn't a major problem; her teachers were pleased that she was going to have the opportunity of spending the week in Paris. Their only stipulation was that she keep a journal of her experiences as "make-up" work for her missed classes. Preston's situation was much more complicated. When I called his school, the dean was uncompromising. He was doing so badly, he certainly didn't deserve a holiday in Paris. I tried to explain to her that this wasn't a holiday; I was going to Paris on business and was taking the children along because they couldn't be left alone.

"Can't he stay with a friend?" she said, her voice quite flat on the telephone.

"He doesn't have a friend in the city," I reminded her. I was angry that she didn't realize we were talking about Thanksgiving week. How was I going to leave him with a friend over a holiday as traditional as Thanksgiving? Even if he had had a friend, I would not have left him. I heard my voice become very formal. "I am not calling to ask permission for Preston to miss classes," I said. "I've called to inform you he is going to miss classes. I am taking him with me to Paris."

When Preston's French teacher learned that he was going, her reaction was more realistic. "Get lost in Paris and find your way back to your hotel," she told him. "Use your French. You know more than you think you do."

So, on the Sunday night before Thanksgiving, we took off for Paris. We'd taken enough overnight flights for me to know the routine. Arrive at the airport an hour before departure. Be sure to have something for the children to nibble on because dinner was always served around midnight, New York time. Our arrival was also routine. Nothing to declare and on to the taxi stand. Arrive at the hotel around eight-thirty in the morning, go to bed immediately to catch up with the jet lag, then, in the afternoon, start exploring the new city.

There was one hitch. The room I had booked for our runaway week was in one of the lesser hotels. When we arrived at around nine that Monday morning, we were told our room would not be available until noon. "I booked for early arrival," I informed the arrogant desk clerk.

"In Paris, sir, rooms are not available until noon."

"And what am I to do with the children until noon?"

"They can have breakfast."

"We have had breakfast. On the plane. I booked for early arrival."

"In Europe, sir—"

"This is not my first trip to Europe. I know that when one books for early arrival, rooms are available in the early morning."

"In Paris, sir—"

"I had had quite enough. I turned, told the children to wait with our luggage and walked out of the hotel. Less than half a block down the street was a hotel I knew, a much more expensive one, but I certainly wasn't going to be intimidated by a desk clerk after an overnight flight.

The Hotel Bedford had a large room immediately available. A young bellboy accompanied me down the street to the other hotel to collect our bags. The children were sitting in the far corner of the lobby, their faces glum. They are always embarrassed when I tangle with desk clerks or dining-room captains—they usually physically separate themselves from me, pretending they don't know me. I suspected there would be a scene, so I sent them along with the bellboy to the Bedford before confronting the clerk.

"We are not staying here," I informed him.

He waved my reservation in my face. "I have a confirmed reservation—for a week," he said triumphantly.

"The reservation was for 'early arrival.' You did not provide the accommodations requested."

"This is a confirmed reservation," he repeated. "I will have to charge you for at least two nights."

"Bill me," I told him and headed for the street.

"Your address, sir."

"In care of the American embassy should do."

A couple of years earlier, Molly had suggested that we tour France on one of our vacations. I told her then the two of them would have to visit France on their own. I had had quite enough of French arrogance in the two years I lived there in the fifties. My encounter with the hotel clerk only reinforced my lingering prejudices.

Our room was on the top floor of the Bedford, with a view of the classic rooftops I so loved. The run-in at the other hotel had revitalized the three of us. Instead of piling into bed for a nap as we had done in the past, we were anxious to see the city.

On the plane I had realized I had made no plans as far as the children were concerned. From Tuesday through Friday I would be busy all day at the conference. They couldn't be left alone in the hotel all day. Although they had never been on their own in a foreign city before, I decided they could probably cope far better than most of the bewildered tourists from Kansas or Kentucky who visit Paris every year. So the first order of business was to make our way to the American Express office to book tours for the next three days.

The Bedford is on the Rue de l'Arcade, within walking distance of the American Express office. After unpacking, we left the hotel and I carefully explained the route we were taking so they could do it on their own. Once there, I booked an afternoon tour of Paris on Tuesday, a day-long trip to Versailles and Fontainebleau on Wednesday and a visit to Chartres on Thursday. I would worry about Friday later.

The day was raw, but the sun was bright and the sky the kind of blue you only see over Paris. I had forgotten how truly beautiful the city is. The only way to appreciate it is to walk its streets.

After leaving American Express, we circled the Opera House and headed down the Avenue de l'Opéra—and into my past. How often I had walked from our hotel, and later our apartment, on the Left Bank to American Express to collect our mail. The three of us paused at the Place du Carrousel while Preston took pictures of the Louvre and the Tuileries, then across the Seine to the Quai Voltaire.

Instinctively, I turned up the Rue Bonaparte to the Rue des Beaux Arts. I pointed out the hotel where their mother and I had lived when we first arrived in Paris. The hotel had seemed romantic then, a small, charming hideaway where I often worked until two or three in the morning on the never-to-be-published novel. In the cold light of a November day, the building looked drab, even shabby. We walked on to the Boulevard St. Germain and the Café Deux Magots, where I had spent many hours so long ago.

"How old were you when you lived here?" Molly asked.

"Thirty-one. Your mother was twenty-six when we came here."

"I can't imagine you that young," she said, her voice trailing off into silence.

"It may be hard to believe, but I was twelve once. For a whole year, I was twelve, like you."

"But you weren't in Paris when you were twelve," Preston added.

"I may have been. There is a small town in Kentucky named Paris. And one named Versailles."

The customers in the café all looked familiar. Not that I remembered any specific face, but the overly made-up lady in a tattered fur coat, a small poodle sitting on her lap; the heavyset man with a large mustache reading *Le Monde*; the young lovers in the corner—all looked the same as the people who frequented the café when I was last there. When I finished my coffee we walked to the Vagenede restaurant for a late lunch, then down to the Rue de Savoie, where their mother and I had an apartment after we returned from our trip to Japan. Like the Rue des

Beaux Arts, Savoie seemed bleak and narrow and unfriendly in the glare of the November sun.

"Boy, you and Mom sure lived in the slums of Paris," Preston observed.

"This isn't a slum, it's just a— When we lived here, it was romantic to have a place on the Left Bank. Artists, writers, creative types. These buildings are several hundred years old."

"They look it."

I had to admit the section looked considerably less romantic than it had when I lived there. The façades of the buildings hadn't changed, I was seeing them with different eyes. We walked on to the Petit Point and across the Seine to Notre Dame. Busloads of Japanese tourists arrived at the same time we did. They poured off the buses and immediately started taking pictures of their friends taking pictures of the cathedral. I sat in a café with a brandy while the children climbed the towers to take pictures of Paris. For two years this city had been my home, and as I sat waiting for the children, I found myself suppressing memories of my life with Vanessa. Flashes of days we spent together would float to the surface, only to be forced down, not dealt with. I was relieved when the children rejoined me. I really didn't want to deal with my earlier experiences in Paris.

After Notre Dame we returned to our hotel for a long nap. Around eight we got dressed and went to Restaurant Lapérouse on the Quai des Grands Augustins, just down the street from the Rue de Savoie, for dinner. We were shown into a small private dining room with a red velvet sofa, two red velvet-covered chairs, red velvet drapes, a hunting scene on the wall. The children laughed a lot, even when things weren't particularly funny. They were happy and relaxed. For the first time since Preston had moved in, we were once again a team, sharing equally a new experience as we had done so many times before.

Molly had been hurt and confused by Preston's decision to live with me. On the weekends she was in, she was defensive, often picking fights with Preston over minor things she would have ignored before. Both children have a strong sense of space. They immediately stake out a chair or the end of a sofa in a hotel room when we travel. In the apartment I usually sat at one end of the sofa, Preston in a chair near the hi-fi so he could listen to his favorite music through earphones. Molly instinctively started sitting either in the chair Preston claimed or at the end of the sofa I normally used. It was as though, through pre-empting our space, she was trying to exert her presence in the apartment. I knew she felt left out, that the two of us now had a life together that did not really include her. In Paris we were on neutral ground again; we were on an equal footing. No one was on the outside.

On Tuesday morning I dressed and slipped out of the room while they were still asleep. I called and woke them up at ten, reminding them of their afternoon tour and making them repeat the directions for getting to the American Express office. They were both in bed when I returned to the hotel in the evening. It was apparent that they had seen more of Paris than they really wanted to see. Both were exhausted from the Sunday-night flight, the long walk on Monday and now the bus tour. We decided to eat in the hotel.

After dinner they were more animated, so I suggested

that we visit a small club I knew. The club, featuring international folk songs, was located on the Rue de l'Abbaye, just behind the Church of St. Germain des Prés. It was owned by two Americans who had become close friends over the years. Nothing had changed in the club, not even Gordon Heath and Lee Payant. There was some gray in their hair, their faces looked more lived in, but they sounded the same.

I introduced the children to my old friends and we sat at the table in the corner where I had sat so many times before. The first song Lee sang was one I had often requested —"Greensleeves." His hard-edged voice was totally right for the song, and as I listened to the familiar lyrics, I was suddenly overcome with emotion. My first reaction was embarrassment, but when I realized I couldn't stop what was happening, I sank back in my chair and listened to Lee sing a song I loved. And then it was as though I were suddenly living in two different time frames simultaneously. Sitting at the same table was a much younger Stafford: lean, wearing a gray tweed jacket and the white turtleneck sweater Rieko had knitted for me just before I left Japan. And a much younger Vanessa was sitting next to me, her tweed suit rough against my hand as I held her arm. I could see both versions of myself. I felt the emotions of the younger man, eager, alive, full of hope, in love as only a newlywed is in love. And the emotions of the older man who has learned to accept the compromise that is life.

In that highly charged moment I realized I had taken the children to the club exactly twenty years to the day Vanessa and I had first met Gordon and Lee. We had landed in Cannes in mid-November, and after a few days in the sun we made our way to Paris. "I want to spend our first Thanksgiving in Paris," Vanessa said. So we arrived on the Monday before Thanksgiving, and on Tuesday night we went to the club. And sat at the same table and listened to the same song.

How differently my life had turned out. I wasn't at all the sort of man I had expected to be, that first night we went to the club. It would never have crossed my mind that fifteen years later my marriage would fall apart, that I would become a part of the business establishment I so distrusted then. The two visions of myself I could see on my mind's film screen seemed alien to each other. But there were so many other days between that moment in 1954 and the present. Had each day been duly recorded or only those few moments when I was totally alive, my mind and my senses in total sync? Surely something has been retained from each of those days and weeks and months and years that, added together, constitute my life. So many years of my existence seem to have grayed with age; they are a vague blur, nothing remembered, no joy, no pain, no moment of being awake. Have I spent most of my life sleepwalking, getting out of bed day after dreary day, mechanically performing the routine that passes for my existence?

I felt drained of energy. Molly slipped her hand into mine and we sat silently as Gordon and Lee finished their program of songs, most familiar, but none charged with the emotional impact of the first. When they were done, we said good night and headed back to our hotel.

When I sat down on the edge of Molly's bed to kiss her good night, she put her arms around my neck. "Did you love Mother a lot?" she asked.

"Yes. We were very much in love when we married."

"But you don't love her anymore?"

Molly had never asked about the divorce and I had made it a policy not to discuss the separation with the children unless they brought it up. During Preston's and my talks we had gone into the reasons for the divorce, but Molly had never seemed to want an explanation.

"Why don't you love her anymore?" she asked because I hadn't answered her first question.

"That's very difficult to answer. People change. I'm not the same person who married your mother twenty years ago. And she isn't the same person. People change over the years."

"How have you changed? How are you different?"

"I'm twenty years older and I expect different things out of life now than I did then."

"What kind of things?"

"Lots of things. I thought when I was younger I could have some impact on the world, that I could do something important. Now I'm content to do my job well and to enjoy each day as it comes along. And to love my children and watch them grow up."

"Are you happy, Dad?"

"Yes. I think I'm happy. Why do you ask?"

"Because you cried tonight. I've never seen you cry before."

"I wasn't crying because I was sad. I cried because I remembered what I was like twenty years ago."

"And you were happy then?"

"Yes. But it was a different kind of happiness. Are you happy?"

"Sometimes. I'm most happy when you take Preston and me to places. Yugoslavia was a happy place. Spain was happy."

"And Paris?"

"So far, it's a happy place. But I was worried when you started to cry. If Mother had come to Paris with us, would you love her again?"

"I don't think so, Molly. Too much has changed, so much has happened. It's nice to remember what was, but that doesn't change what is."

"You and Mother will never live together again?"

Preston had asked the same question when he was twelve. And I had told him the same thing I had to tell Molly. If you have loved someone intensely, with as much concern and respect as you can pull together, and that love turns sour, there is no way to rekindle the flame. I was aware of Molly's unspoken fears; if I could no longer love her mother, could I also arrive at a point where I might no longer love her?

"Molly, the love between a man and his wife is different from the love a father has for his children. Do you understand that?"

"I'm not sure."

"What I'm trying to say is that I will always love you and Preston. My love for you has nothing to do with the kind of love I had for your mother. I know it is difficult to understand. It's certainly difficult to explain. But know that I will always love you. And I want you to have a happy time in Paris. Okay?"

She pulled away from me for a moment, then put her head on my knee. "Dad, why did you ask Preston to live with you and not ask me?"

My God, she thought I had asked her brother to move in! "I didn't ask Preston to live with me, Molly. Preston told me he wanted to live with me and your mother agreed. Molly, don't feel I love Preston more than I love you."

"When did Preston ask to live with you?"

"When he was eleven. I told him that when he was fourteen, and if he still wanted to live with me, I'd do what I could."

"He never told me he had asked to live with you."

"I guess it was a secret just between the two of us. Are you terribly upset that he moved in?"

"Nothing's the same anymore. If I want to move in when I'm fourteen, can I?"

"If you really want to, I'll do everything I can. Sure."

And I had committed myself again. But I couldn't tell her I thought that, being a girl, she should stay with her mother. That it was difficult enough for me to care for Preston, but that it would be even harder to have the responsibilities of a teen-age daughter. I ran my fingers through her long brown hair. "We'll talk about it later, okay? It's late and you have to catch a bus at nine tomorrow morning."

"Did you and Mother ever go on a bus tour of Versailles?"

"No. As a matter of fact, I have to confess I've never been to Versailles."

"Then why are we going?"

"I should have gone. It's something you should see. When I was traveling with your mother, I hated cathedrals and castles and museums. I've learned to enjoy them when we travel. I'm catching up on something I should have done before. Go to sleep."

I turned out the lights and took my journal into the

bathroom so I wouldn't disturb the children. It had been an extraordinary day.

Wednesday morning broke cold and wet. After breakfast I bundled up the children and sent them off in the rain to American Express. The international conference, our reason to be in Paris, was being held in a building on the edge of the Bois de Boulogne. It was rush hour and the traffic circling L'Étoile was maddening—how often I had gotten stuck in an inner lane and lacked the courage to dart through the rushing cars to the avenue I was heading for! Once I circled the damn Arc six times before I summoned up the courage to bully my way through the traffic to the exit I wanted. My taxi driver was more adept than I. He had a loud voice, an unpleasant hand gesture and nerves of steel.

The conference itself consisted of endless hours of banal ambiguities. Since most of the people with something they felt compelled to share represented non-English-speaking countries, I listened to the sleep-inducing drone of interpreters through the earphones. After the first day I learned to put the earphones on and turn off the volume. I sat hour after exasperating hour, with what I hoped was an interested expression on my face while my mind roamed through much more interesting subjects.

The trip to Paris had come at a most crucial time for the children and me. The two months since Preston had moved in had been very difficult for all of us. Aside from having to adjust to a new and very demanding school, Preston had also had to deal with his sense of guilt for having walked out on Molly, who obviously felt abandoned, first by her father and now by her brother. She suspected the life Preston and I were living was somehow better, easier, more carefree than the one she was leading. She was resentful and often moody. And for me . . .

Sitting with my silent earphones, I tried to figure out whether or not Preston's move had been at all wise. He certainly wasn't doing well in school, he was becoming remote in his relationship with me. We had conquered the household routines everyone had warned me about, but we hadn't even touched on the deeper, more important problems of the transition. Paris was giving us an opportunity, at a difficult period in our lives, to separate ourselves from our normal routines and to experience our relationship without the tugs of time schedules and household chores.

I spent Thursday, Thanksgiving Day in America but a working day in Europe, dealing with the clutter floating around in my mind. I was fifty. My career was set. Nothing new or unexpected could be in the cards for me. The young man I had briefly experienced at the club on Tuesday night was long gone. His dreams, his hopes, his commitments were from the past. But I realized I was still feeling guilty because of those commitments. He was still haunting me, refusing to allow me to enjoy the present because I hadn't lived up to the expectations of my youth. There was nothing really wrong with my present. I had a failed marriage, but that certainly wasn't unique. My career wasn't spectacular, but I had made a conscious decision not to claw my way to the top the way most of my "successful" friends had done. And I had something I had never really properly appraised before. I had two really fantastic children. The young man sitting in the Club L'Abbaye twenty years before would never have thought that the meaning of life was children you love and respect. There was a surprising inner calm, almost an inner warmth, which came over me when I finally faced the reality of my life. What had I to complain about? For heaven's sake, I was making a decent living in a job that did not require me to sell a slice of my soul every day and I had two wonderful children. My life wasn't a waste; I was much better off than most of my friends.

I was awakened from my reveries when everyone started taking off their earphones and pushing their chairs away from the long conference table. "Are you joining us for Thanksgiving dinner?" another American at the conference asked. "At the American embassy. You and your children are invited."

"I'm sorry, I've made other plans," I told her. What I didn't tell her was that I really needed to spend the time alone with my children. At this point in our lives we needed to share something very personal, not an official function which would require our party manners. I had made reservations at Fouquet's.

By this time Molly and Preston had spent three days together, totally dependent on each other. Their experiences poured out as we sat in Fouquet's . . . dining on chicken, not turkey. Molly told me about the confused American tourist who could not deal with francs on the trip to Versailles. Preston was very optimistic about the pictures he had taken at Chartres. Each had a tale to tell, each reinforcing the other, embellishing the other's stories. It was a Thanksgiving to remember, and in the back of my mind I kept trying to recall the first Thanksgiving I had spent in Paris with Vanessa—and couldn't. What restaurant had we gone to? Did we have fun? Nothing had been recorded in my mind, at least nothing I could project on the screen I now knew existed in my head. Another of those lost days that make up my life.

My plan for Friday was simple. They were tired and bored with bus tours, so they were assigned to wander through the shops on the Rue Saint Honoré and the Rue de Rivoli to find Christmas gifts. They were to take along a notebook, and list prices and locations of shops which we would return to on Saturday after the conference had ended. When I returned to the hotel on Friday night I found they had: 1) made a thorough search for the shops offering what they wanted to buy, and 2) gotten lost. Preston's assignment had been completed, for they obviously made it back to the hotel using his limited knowledge of French.

It was raining lightly on Saturday, but we didn't really care. We retraced their steps and bought everyone's Christmas present, including some herbs for their mother at a special shop near the Madeleine which I hoped the customs officials wouldn't think was "grass" when we returned to New York.

There was a mood of sadness on Saturday night. The week had been emotionally intense for all of us. "I don't want to go home," Molly said when we were having dinner in a café near the hotel.

"I don't either," Preston added.

I didn't either. I didn't want to go back into the pressures we had left behind us. I did know, however, more about myself than I had ever known before. That moment of awareness had cleared away a lot of fog in my mind. We were going to be all right, the three of us. Somehow it was going to work out fine. I didn't have any new answers but I was more confident I could somehow pull it off. I hadn't sacrificed Molly's love by allowing Preston to move in. She had been damaged, but she was salvageable. All three of us held hands as we walked in the rain back to the hotel.

The children went immediately to bed and I did something I had never done before in a Paris bar—or any bar, for that matter. I ordered a bottle of champagne and sat alone, sipping the wine and storing up memories of our week in Paris. How fragile life is, how fleeting. How difficult to pin down a moment, a day. Tomorrow I would have to face customs, immigration, airline clerks, taxi drivers, but for one fleeting moment I knew who I was and I knew that my existence depended on the relationship I had with both my children. This was my life. The trip to Paris was worth every cent it would cost when the bills from my credit cards started arriving.

XI

The sense of well-being which had settled over the three of us in Paris slowly dissolved in the gray, cold days of December in New York. Preston plunged back into his school work with grim determination, his sense of humor once again buried under the load of facts needing remembering, reports past due. Since I could do nothing about his math problems, I volunteered to type his history and English reports. There was one stumbling block—I couldn't read his handwriting. He would have to dictate his report to me, I would do a rough draft and he would correct spelling and punctuation. Anything not corrected on the draft went into the final version, to be graded accordingly.

It was through these sometimes long and painful evenings that Preston and I began to establish a different kind of relationship. I was intrigued by how his mind worked, how he dealt with his assignments. Sometimes I would insist that he go back and start all over again; I couldn't tell him what was wrong, only point out that something needed a new approach, more facts. Often his frustration reduced him to a string of words he had, I'm afraid, learned from me. But there were no longer evenings of evasion. I was involved enough in his day-to-day projects to know what was going on. There were times when I felt as though I were repeating my own freshman year, sometimes irritable because I was, to use an Army expression, over age in grade. I already knew the dates of World War II, I had served in it, and constantly had to remind myself that Preston was dealing with what was past history for him, not my own experiences.

The heaviness of our life was beginning to be offset by moments of levity. "The kids at school can't believe I live with my father," Preston said one night at dinner.

"What's wrong with your living with me?"

"They think it's crazy."

"Are any of their parents divorced?"

"Are you kidding? But they live with their mothers. One guy said he wouldn't want to live with his father. He asked me what we talked about. He never talks with his father."

"What did you tell him?"

"We talk about everything. That you're interested in politics and history and we talked about it. And football. Things like that. One guy who doesn't see much of his father said it might be fun. When he does see his father, they always go to baseball games and eat in nice restaurants. His mother never takes him to restaurants."

Preston's peers weren't the only ones who found it difficult to believe his life with me was not really any different than it would be if he were living with his mother. The mail from the school administration was always addressed to "Mrs. Stafford." If permission was necessary for some activity, he was always told to have his mother write a note.

Calls from various volunteer groups always asked for "Mrs. Stafford." There would be an embarrassed pause on the other end of the line when I informed the caller that Preston and I lived alone.

Our life style baffled everyone who knew of the arrangement. After several months Preston and I established ourselves as steady customers at the supermarket. We became Saturday-morning friends of a middle-aged lady at the check-out counter. One rainy morning she was ringing up our heavily laden cart when she suddenly stopped and stuck a bag of flour in my face. "Are you sure your wife had this on her list?"

"I don't understand," I muttered.

"Are you sure she wanted this, not all-purpose flour?"

"Is there a difference?" I knew there was a difference, but I had been careless and picked up the wrong bag.

"Of course there is. Let me see your list."

"I haven't a list." Preston exchanged the bag as she continued to check us out. "I don't have a wife," I told the nice lady.

"But you and the boy are in here every week."

"We live together. My son and I." The people in line behind us were beginning to sound restless. I went back to packing the orange juice and milk and packages of frozen vegetables.

"Just you and the boy?" she asked, muttering something in Spanish under her breath.

"Right."

"Next time, don't buy this," she said, holding up a package of margarine. "[XX] is just as good and cheaper. And don't buy this either. Man, I thought what a crazy wife you have and you don't have a wife."

"Guess I'm the one who's crazy."

"No. You're just a man. But the boy looks healthy."

After that rainy morning I always waited in her line, regardless of how long it was. She would do things that never occurred to me—checking the boxes to see they weren't damaged, making sure I was taking advantage of what was on sale that week. It wasn't that I was incapable of taking care of myself. But I can't stand supermarkets and try to get the whole thing over as rapidly as possible. In my haste I often make mistakes. Anyway, a clever shopper's eye doesn't hurt and I actually think she enjoys monitoring my efforts. Because of her, I became a much better bargain hunter. She always had a warm greeting for Preston and commented on how he was growing. (Had he grown as much from week to week as her comments indicated, he would soon have qualified for a spot with the NETS.) And I would watch her face go blank as she turned to the next customer, a harried young mother with a toddler riding in the jump seat of the shopping cart. Zip, zip, zip. No comment. Women could take care of themselves, but men . . .

The people in the dry-cleaning shop were slow to become aware there had been a permanent addition to my household. One evening in late winter when I stopped by for my shirts, the owner asked, "Is your boy living with you now? He's been in and out a lot recently."

"Yes. He's moved in with me."

"How do you manage?"

"Fairly well, thank you."

"You know, if you have any mending, that sort of thing . . . I mean, my seamstress can help out."

I appreciated his gesture but decided not to tell him I had spent the last evening turning up a new pair of pants and sewing a couple of missing buttons on a shirt.

My landlord inquired of my son's health every time we met in the lobby. Being a bachelor, he must have felt my life was difficult at best because I was caring for a teen-age boy.

The neighborhood concern for our well-being was comforting—and amusing. Everyone knows a male isn't capable of child care, so they were pitching in. But things were going much better than I had thought they would.

Outside our immediate community, things were not quite so simple. Many of the people I knew socially could not understand that I was no longer available at a moment's notice to stop by for drinks, to attend this or that affair, and by early spring the phone had stopped ringing. I was no longer another available male for a party. I found I didn't care that I had been dropped from various social lists. I was enjoying my new life and didn't need to dash from party to party to keep myself amused.

The reaction of my professional associates struck me as extremely odd. The men who over the years had complained bitterly about the way the ex-wife was caring for their children never once hinted they wished their children were living with them. A wall of silence surrounded the subject of child care. There were no more complaints about what was or was not going on in the house in the suburbs. I suspected my actions had made them feel guilty. I had proved a man could adequately care for his son, so they were faced with the reality that they really didn't want to take on the responsibility of their own children.

The truth was out in the open and the only way they could deal with it was to ignore the whole subject.

My women friends were openly hostile on the subject. If they discussed it at all, it was in sarcastic tones. It was as though my actions had somehow threatened them. I wanted to assure them I was not the spearhead of an advancing horde of fathers who were going to demand equal rights as far as their children were concerned. I knew something they didn't . . . their ex-husbands were quite content to let them care for the kids. They had nothing to fear. My generation has been too brainwashed, too conditioned by their mothers and society in general to even consider changing the status quo. I know, because I was one of them until Preston took matters in his own hands.

The single exception to the hands-off position of my associates was Clara, a young woman whom I've known professionally for a number of years. When we first met she was secretary to a documentary-film producer. Now she is a producer in her own right. It had been several years since our paths crossed, and a number of things had happened in her life. One of them was disillusionment in her career. Being a producer was not as glamorous as she once thought it would be.

Viewed from below, the rooms at the top represent success, power, money. The Great American Dream. But they also represent frustration, isolation, tension. Lined up outside the door to every one of those rooms are five or more young, talented, ambitious tigers waiting to pounce if you falter, as you pounced to get there in the first place. Clara probably made an even greater sacrifice than her male counterparts, but the end result is the same. She is trapped by her success. The numbness of the spirit had already set in; she was slowly becoming aware that the power and the prestige and excitement of having arrived had cost her a great chunk of her soul. She also knew something the women who were bored with the routine of child care and housework never suspected—that there was also a deadly sameness to the jobs their husbands went off to every morning. She no longer looked with envy at the male world.

Clara's marriage is the reverse of the usual domestic scene. Her husband, Paul, is an artist who works at home. He is talented, but he has yet to make his name in a most difficult field. So when they decided to have a child, it was Paul's job to take over the nurturing chores, to take the boy to the park and to birthday parties and the checkups at the doctor. It was the mother who arrived home too exhausted to want to play with her son, too frustrated from having spent her day on the wheel in the hamster cage she thinks of as her career to really involve herself in her child's life.

"At first I thought it was just me," she said. "Maybe because I was a woman, everything was different. But it isn't just me. The men I've talked to feel the same way."

"Why don't you get out?"

"I can't. I'm trapped. Just like the guy in the office next to mine and the guy in the office next to him. I've got to make a living. Paul doesn't earn enough . . ." Her voice trailed off into her martini glass.

"Trapped by your standard of living."

"Right. And something else. I've worked so damn hard to get where I am. I just can't walk away. I haven't the courage. I know I'm missing a lot not being around while Jeff is growing up, but it's too late to think about that."

"From all I've read, you should be relieved not to be a houseslave. Deadly boring, just being a wife and mother."

"You know, Paul never complains about being bored taking care of Jeff. He's really turned on by kids. I'm not sure I would have done as good a job as he has. Do you find taking care of your son a bore?"

"Just the opposite. I was terrified at first, but I came to the whole thing late in the game, not like Paul. My generation is different than yours, as I suppose you've noticed."

I felt sorry for Clara. She had competed in the "male" world and succeeded, only to find her success bittersweet. She had willingly agreed to have Paul's child, knowing she did not relish the role of motherhood. She was caught in the middle, her life a series of frustrations. She loves and respects Paul, she loves her son and often feels guilty for not being more involved in his life. Unfortunately she can't have life both ways; she can't spend weeks at a time on the road with a film crew and still be intimately involved in Jeff's growing up. She is like so many fathers who spend most of their waking hours struggling to maintain a life style they have little time to enjoy.

Little Jeff, however, is much more fortunate than many children I know. Paul is an excellent "mother." He does not consider himself a slave to the child, the way so many women feel these days. As a result the boy is open and free and responsive to adults. He has not been denied the nurturing he needed to develop into an emotionally and physically healthy child.

And the nurturing during those early, demanding years came from a male.

"What's the reaction of your friends?" Clara asked.

"I actually think everyone wants me to fall flat on my face. It must be much worse for Paul."

It wasn't until I was talking with Clara that I remembered what it had been like, fourteen years earlier, when I took my tiny son to the park. The bench sitters in 1960 were, I'm sure, quite different from the harried mothers of the middle seventies. Motherhood was still a fairly respectable career then. The conversations I overheard concerned Dr. Spock rather than Betty Friedan. One thing, however, has remained the same. The male in charge of a tiny baby is made to feel out of place among the pram crowd in the park. Regardless of how much the ladies may resent their plight, I seriously question if any of them would admit that either me in the sixties or Paul in the seventies could properly care for a young child. In my case, I was sitting in the park because it had to be done, and I would certainly have agreed that child care was the woman's role. Paul was there because he chose to care for his son and really didn't give a damn what they thought. But Paul had to be some kind of a nut. There is, apparently, something quite strange about a man who wants to care for his children.

And Clara has to be considered somewhat strange, at least by the women of my generation. It is perfectly proper to turn over the care of children to maids, but to allow the father to take over is considered abnormal. If Paul and Clara's marriage should fail, there would be no question of who would have custody of the boy. Clara, although she was Jeff's mother, did not feel she "owned" him.

Paul and Clara's arrangement isn't the only role-reversal marriage I have known. The first summer after the separation, when I took the children to Puerto Rico, we met a couple who thought the same way. However, at the time I had no understanding of what was going on. I was still in a state of shock and too bewildered by my own feeling of inadequacy to appreciate what I was observing. My journal entry the night after I met them was cryptic and condescending. "Very strange couple. Dick is in complete charge of the little girl. What kind of a woman is Dorothy anyway, expecting Dick to care for the girl? And what kind of a man is Dick? Sometimes I thought I was henpecked, but nothing like this."

The vacation was nearly over when I met them. One day I noticed a young man with a sleeping child in one of those carrying packs on his back coming down the beach. He spread a blanket under the shade of a tree, put the child down and stretched out beside it. When the child woke up and began to cry, he put his book down and devoted his full attention to amusing the little girl. Before long both of my children had joined him, and the four of them went into the water. The baby wasn't old enough to walk. The father sat her at the edge of the surf, where she splashed with glee every time a wave washed the shore. When it was time for us to go back up to the apartment for lunch, I called the children.

"Can they join us for lunch?" Molly asked. "His name is Dick and the baby's name is Elana. Please, can they come up for lunch?"

Dick accepted my invitation and all of us went upstairs. The children played with the baby in the living room while Dick helped me fix sandwiches. It struck me as odd that he would be alone with a child so young—not more than eight months old. I knew why I was alone with my two, but surely he wasn't vacationing with a child as young as Elana. As it turned out, the child's mother was around the point in an apartment where she was working on her thesis for a doctorate in literature. He kept the baby out of the apartment as much as he could so that she could get her work done. It seemed a considerate thing for him to do and I thought no more about it until the next evening when I invited him to stop by for drinks with his wife. Throughout the evening, Dorothy had nothing to do with the child. It was Dick who changed her when she cried, who fixed her bottle and put her down on Molly's bed in the other room.

They were both very interesting people. Dick was working on a novel and Dorothy hoped to complete her doctorate within a few months. She taught English literature at a college in upstate New York. It had been weeks since I had had a chance to talk about anything except how to fold laundry and bake chicken. It was a most pleasant evening. As they were leaving, Dick suggested that the following night the two of us drive to the casino down the beach. Dorothy agreed to baby-sit with the three children—she had a lot of reading to do and wouldn't mind being alone.

I have often tried to reconstruct the conversation that we had at the bar after both of us had blown all the money we felt we could afford to lose. I can't remember what led up to the point where I asked the question I had no right to put. "Why are you the only one taking care of your daughter?" I heard myself asking.

"What do you mean?"

"I mean that you are totally in charge of your daughter. You feed, change, bathe her, take her to the beach."

"She is my daughter," he answered in the tone of voice that didn't invite another question. Dick was a tall man, with hefty shoulders and dark-brown hair that fell over his collar. He played with the ice in his drink for a moment, then said, almost as an afterthought, "Our daughter. Dorothy is her mother."

"It occurred to me she might be your daughter from another marriage."

"No. Our daughter." And he explained the situation very simply. "Dorothy and I met while we were working in the Peace Corps. We started living together and when we returned to the States, we decided to get married. But I made one condition. I wanted to have children. I'd learned something about children and about myself while working in India. And I wanted my own. She didn't want children, so we split up for a while. But I loved her and she loved me. So I told her that if she would have my children, I would care for them. She wouldn't be stuck with them. We have a pact. I have the kind of job where I'm free most of the day. I'm a dorm master and when I have to be out, I can get one of the students to baby-sit. She's free to teach and take courses and I have time to work on my book. It's working out nicely for both of us. Isn't the kid great?"

We were sitting in heavy mock leather chairs in a bar decorated in an unholy mixture of early M-G-M and insecure W. & J. Sloane's. Our conversation seemed out of place. We should have been discussing golf scores or the stock market.

"Did you want them. Your kids?" he asked me.

"Not before they were born," I confessed. "Having children was not my idea."

"That's what it's all about, you know. Loving kids. Watching them grow up. Sharing their lives. That's where it's all at. All the rest is a crock of shit."

Sitting in the bar that night, he was both at home and out of place. I tried to tell myself that the difference in our attitudes toward children was in the generation gap. He was fifteen years younger than I. But that wasn't the real answer. As I look back I realize he had found out something about life that it took me years longer to find. He already knew at his age that all the rest is a crock. It would never have occurred to me that, four years later, my son would move in with me.

I had put Dick out of my mind until the lunch with Clara. Dick and Paul had a great deal in common. Both creative, sensitive young men who had decided not to be caught up in the vulgarity of the Great American Dream. Possibly there was some hope for the generation between mine and my children's. Young men in their thirties whose values have been shaped by the Vietnam war and the women's liberation movement, men who could free themselves from outworn cultural myths and seek and maybe find a solid basis for their lives. Maybe they could rediscover the sense of generation, of commitment to their children that would give meaning to their existence.

By late spring I knew I had found a kind of happiness that had always eluded me before. Not the happiness built on the sexual tensions of a romantic affair I'd known with my lovely friend in Japan or the first years of my marriage. A different kind of happiness. A contentment, a sense of dimension, of proportion in my life. During this period I ran across a quote from Pascal in an old journal I had kept when I was living in Paris.

> When I consider the brief span of my life, swallowed up in the eternity before and behind it, the small space that I fill, or even see, engulfed in the infinite immensity of spaces which I know not, and which know not me, I am afraid, and wonder to see myself here rather than there; for there is no reason why I should be here rather than there; now rather than then . . .

Over the years I had forgotten the quote, but its meaning had haunted my existence. Out of some ill-defined existential fear, I had been running, always running, never standing still long enough to be aware of the now of my life. I sensed it was possible for me to stand still for a moment, to live life day by day without that terrible fear of tomorrow, for somehow, life had taken on a new and satisfying direction.

In early June the inevitable happened. Preston was spending the weekend with Molly at their mother's. The phone rang late Saturday afternoon. It was a collect call.

"Dad, Molly wants to talk with you. She's decided to move in with us when she's fourteen."

"But that's a year away."

"She said she could wait a year. I waited longer than that. It's going to be all right, isn't it?"

"Let's discuss it next weekend when she comes in, okay? Sure, tell her it will be all right."

XII

After a few months of living with Preston, I realized we were emotionally surprisingly alike—both of us content to spend long hours alone with a book, needing few close friends. "I'm not very social," Preston protested when I suggested he invite friends over during the weekends. "I see enough of the people I know during the week, I don't need to see them on weekends." The relationship which was emerging was not a typical father/son arrangement. There was no necessity for me to dominate, to dictate; I always knew where he was, for he called if he was going to be late. His calling wasn't because I ordered it, but because he respected the fact that I would be worried. But we were not, on the other hand, buddy-buddies. I was still his father and expected him to take my wishes seriously.

The peer-group pressures on Preston to succeed, to challenge, to "be a man" were depressingly similar to the ones I suffered through. The social revolution which is altering the road map of American life has yet to deal with the group pressures on teen-age boys, at least not in the school

Preston attends. But then, the liberation movement apparently has not concerned itself constructively with the rights of children; quite the opposite, it would appear that the movement is basically anti-children, especially male children.

I could bring personal experience to my understanding of Preston's problems. But Molly's problems were going to be a lot different and very little in my experience was going to help. I knew there was going to be much I would have to learn, things that are, at least for me, part of a deep, mysterious cult women never share with men, not with husbands and fathers and brothers at any rate. I would have to try to understand something about the cult of the female body if I was to successfully deal with my teen-age daughter.

It wasn't until there seemed to be a real possibility that Molly would live with me that I paid more than passing attention to the literature written by women primarily for women. When the writer is dealing with the public life of women—equal pay for equal work, equal opportunity for advancement—I feel on firm ground, for I totally agree with the protesters. I have always preferred the company of intelligent, forceful women to the simpering nitwits who use their charms to weave a spider web to entrap an equally nitwit male. I can also understand to some degree women who find child care confining, housework unrewarding. Some women are simply not constitutionally geared to the demands of child care, and their resentment affects not only their own life but the life of their children. If a woman does not find satisfaction in being a part of the growing up and development of a child, she should not be forced to go through it—or to be made to feel guilty if she prefers a different life style.

So far, so good. But I was unprepared for the charges that the male was guilty of brutalizing the female body. During my lifetime I have shared the collective guilt for events I did not participate in or cause to happen. As a WASP I experienced guilt because of what the German madman did to Jews. As a Southerner I could not easily dismiss the guilt of my ancestors—and contemporaries—for the treatment of blacks in this country. As a political liberal I cannot accept the reality that millions of children go to bed hungry while others have more food on their plates than they can eat. By nature I seem to have a guilt-ridden Protestant soul. However, as I pored over books on the liberation movement, I found that I, personally, did not feel guilty as a male because women had menstrual cycles or because birth was painful. The writers in so many cases were blaming the male for a condition which is biological, not social. As an individual I have never raped or brutalized a woman. As a husband I impregnated my wife, who had two very difficult experiences giving birth. But I was not in any way responsible for the physical make-up of the woman who was my wife. Nor had I forced my wife to become a mother. That decision had been hers, not mine. I certainly wasn't prepared for statements such as Adrienne Rich made in her book *Of Woman Born*:

> Throughout patriarchal mythology, dream-symbolism, theology, language, two ideas flow side by side: one, that the female body is impure, corrupt, the side of discharges, bleedings, dangerous to masculinity, a source of moral and physical contamination, "the devil's gateway."

On the other hand, as mother the woman is beneficent, sacred, pure, asexual, nourishing; and the physical potential for motherhood—that same body with its bleedings and mysteries—is her single destiny and justification in life. These two ideas have become deeply internalized in women, even in the most independent of us, those who seem to lead the freest lives.

Writer after writer detailed the degradation of being a woman, of how men used women's reproductive powers to control them, the religious rites males had established to purify the impure female. Through personal experience I have long been aware of some of the taboos regarding the menstrual cycle. While living with my friend Rieko in Japan, I learned that a woman could not walk through a torii gate while she was having her period.

"Then why did you just do it?" I asked Rieko after we entered a Shinto shrine.

"It's a silly custom. Only old women would think anything about it."

Rieko was a Shinto. All noble families in Japan are Shinto, and her cousin, a prince until the new constitution drafted by Americans wiped out all titles other than the immediate royal family, was head priest of the shrine we were visiting.

"What would your cousin think?" I asked her.

"In public, he would say it is a religious law. In private, he would laugh."

Oriental women, as far as popular fiction is concerned, are among the world's most oppressed. The Japanese women I knew were years ahead of their American counterparts. I must qualify that statement: the Japanese women I knew through Rieko represented a small percentage of the population, the once noble families and daughters of the industrial elite. But these women were liberated in a land where it is customary to think of all females as slaves to their husbands. After producing an heir, they did pretty much as they pleased. The women I knew had male "secretaries"—young, handsome men who accompanied them wherever they went, including their bedchambers.

These Japanese women were liberated without that heavy weight of guilt and anger I found in books written by American women. Rieko ignored menstrual taboos without thinking of herself as a revolutionary. She was simply a woman doing what she wanted to do. She thought of herself as a person capable of accepting and giving love with her body. Her body wasn't a biological anchor; rather it was a source of pleasure for her—and for me.

The more I read of the female's anguish for having been born female, the less I felt a part of the collective guilt the female wishes the male to assume. Yes, women absolutely must be treated equally in the business world and in all family matters. But as a twentieth-century male, who had nothing to do with the formation of the myths of Adam and Eve and the rest of the cultural symbolism I found in the books on feminism, there is nothing I can do about their biological condition. What struck me was that the writers appeared to believe those myths still have an influence on men today. No male I know thinks of a woman's menstrual cycle as anything other than a routine bodily function. There is no mystery, no occult meaning attached to it, no sense of evil or disgust. I am fully aware there are men who beat their wives, but not because they are trying to seek revenge on a woman for being a woman. They are psychologically ill men, just as the women who spend most of their lives emotionally castrating their husbands are mentally ill. Such aberrations are not part of the mainstream of our culture; they are just that, aberrations. A man who was beaten by his mother or father will beat his wife or their children, as a woman who was beaten by her father or mother will beat her children and her husband if he isn't physically stronger than she.

(A recent survey reveals that husband beating is one of the least understood, and least reported, crimes in America today. An estimated 200,000 husbands are victims of physical abuse every year. Very, very few males in our *macho* society would dare admit to anyone that the bruise on his face was inflicted by his wife. Psychologically, it must be even more damaging for a male to be subjected to such physical abuse than, say, a battered wife. Society feels sorry for a battered wife—but only contempt for a battered husband.)

Another point struck me as I waded through the literature: there was no real mention of the possibility of affection for the male, no sense of sharing of mutual fears and expectations and hopes. There seemed to be no real understanding of where the American male is today, what drives him on, makes him push harder and harder to arrive at the top of his profession, only to find his success hollow, meaningless. And when he finally does arrive, he learns he has sacrificed the one real reason for having made the effort in the first place—his wife and children. The only function he has retained in his struggle for success is his ability to pay bills. He has become, as far as the liberated women's literature is concerned, obsolete. Obviously something has gone wrong in the male-female relationship. The male must assume half of the responsibility for the breakdown in communication, but we should also expect some understanding of the fact that we are just as much a victim of our culture as our wives or lovers. It wasn't because we thought of our wives as inferior human beings, as "conjugal slaves." We were doing it for them because they let us know they expected it from us. And we came home tired and frightened and insecure and possibly did commit, as one writer insisted, "marital rape." It was a chilling education for me.

One thing was clear. My relationship with Molly had to be one where she would learn that the male can, and in most cases does, respect the rights of the female. I wanted her to respect her body, not to resent it; to accept her bodily functions without feeling nature had played a dirty trick on her. She should expect to be treated as an equal, both in business and in bed, and if she didn't feel she was being treated equally in either, she should move on. Specifically, she should be taught that the male has as many problems adjusting to our society as the female, and only through some mutual effort at understanding each other's problems will anything ever be solved. It was going to be an interesting experience for both of us.

Both the children and I went on the assumption Molly would, indeed, move in the next year. There was no point sharing with them my real concern that this time I was not going to gain custody without a court battle. Preston's situation was different. It was obvious to both his mother and me that I was, and had been all along, his "primary" parent. It is quite normal for a child to feel closer to one parent than the other for a number of subtle emotional reasons. Preston and I always had that kind of emotional rapport.

Molly's situation was quite different. She wasn't really choosing between parents, she was choosing to live with her brother, who happened to live with her father. During the years following the separation Preston had been her anchor, the one real constant in her life. I never for a moment thought she didn't love me and wanted to be with me. But I was fully aware that if Preston had remained in the country with his mother, she would not have initiated the move as he had done. Considering the circumstances—Preston's first visit to the country in a long time and the collect phone call—I had the strong suspicion she had been talked into making the request by her brother. That didn't matter to me. I desperately wanted her to live with us and I was going to do everything possible to make it happen. However, I knew I had to see to it that Molly understood the gravity of what she was doing. This could not be a casual decision. Her mother's hurt, her feeling of rejection, would permanently alter any relationship the two of them would have in the future.

During the first year Preston lived in the city, Molly's weekends were always something special. After those first couple of months when everything had been rather sticky, she came into the city to have fun, to be with her brother and her father. For her, they were a "vacation" from her normal routine. The first thing I did after the request to join Preston was to include her in the routines of our life. She was assigned chores, as Preston had chores. Her first reaction was one of resentment. "But you are going to be living here," I told her when she protested having to help with the dishes. "I do them all the time at home," she insisted. "This is my vacation."

"This is going to be your home and dishes have to be done."

I also included her in the usual weekend activities of getting the laundry out, the shopping done and put away —things she had been spared. I wanted her to know life in the city was not unlike life in the country. Living with Preston and me would mean participating in the unpleasant but necessary functions no one I know particularly enjoys. After the first weekend of being included in the chores, she never protested again. I felt we were over the first hurdle. I also became less willing to give in to her demands, whatever they might be, to see this or that movie, to dine out or stay in. For a year she had been a privileged guest; I had made many concessions because I felt guilty she was still in the country. We were to deal on an equal basis. She responded positively to each challenge. She never wavered in her desire to move in.

As I went through the books on the new American female, I also tried to find some legal rock I could stand on when it came time to actually make the move. All I found was quicksand. Of the millions of divorces over the past few years, less than 5 percent of the males involved gained custody of their children. And as far as I could learn, this pathetically small percentage gained custody because of extreme circumstances—a totally unfit mother. I had no extreme circumstances. All I had was a thirteen-year-old, going on fourteen, who wanted to live with her brother and her father. But she could not, and would not, I'm sure, say anything to a judge which would in any way have embarrassed her mother. She didn't want to hurt her mother, she told me one night when she broke down in tears. She loved her mother but preferred to live with me.

As an expert witness, she was going to be a bust if we went to court. One side of me was very proud of her. She was making a very difficult decision, one I knew was costing her a lot of pain. But she had made it and nothing I said, no vague allusion to the fact that she might want to remain with her mother, that life in the city wasn't a holiday, altered anything. She was moving in as soon as school was out.

Out of respect for my friend and lawyer who had handled my divorce but wanted no part of a brutal court battle over custody, I turned to a young talented man who specializes in "maritals." My first interview with him left me limp. I knew he thought I was stupid to fight for my daughter. "How in hell are you going to be able to take care of her?" he asked me.

"I've done a pretty good job with my son. I can handle it."

"But why?"

I really couldn't explain why. It sounded too simplistic. I loved both my children, I knew I could care for them, and I thought they should be together, regardless of what it might cost both financially and in the hurt of adults. Their lives were more important than any other consideration. We had to proceed. Since we had almost a year, he told me he would give it thought and would come up with something. He was the kind of lawyer one trusts. There was an air of self-confidence about him, a determination to win, even if he thought what I was doing was slightly batty.

In the meantime, there were other matters to attend to. I

was much better informed about schools and wasn't worried about that. The main problem was living space. Preston and I could share a bedroom—and even that arrangement had reached the point where I knew we had to move. Just before Molly informed me that she was moving in, I had started looking for a two-bedroom apartment. Suddenly I was looking for a three-bedroom. I would have to find something before spring, but the available apartments large enough to hold us were either as dark as the tiny one I had first rented after the separation or so expensive I couldn't afford them. Again my landlord, who was concerned about the welfare of my son, came through. There was a three-bedroom apartment opening up in my building in December. I wouldn't have the expense of a moving company, an agent's fee—and all the other costs of moving a household.

I was afraid that Vanessa would be tipped off when she learned I was moving into a larger apartment, but there was no reaction. I kept my fingers crossed. The physical move was scheduled for a weekend Molly was to be in town. The three of us lugged the boxes and beds and sofa and chairs to the service elevator and up two floors to our new home . . . the home all three of us would be sharing come spring.

For the first time in many years I had a kitchen large enough to move around in, two bathrooms so Preston and I didn't have to take turns shaving. And a room for Molly. By spreading out the furniture we had crammed into the other apartment, there was enough for Preston's and my rooms, but only a bed for Molly's. I knew she must feel a part of our life even before she moved in, so I took her shopping for a desk and chair and a dresser and curtains for her windows. By having a room of her own, Molly's attitude toward the city shifted radically. She had the same sense of having a "home" that Preston had felt when I'd first moved into the larger place downstairs. Each of us now had a space that was our own, rooms where doors could be closed, where we could be alone if we wanted to. It wasn't until we moved that I realized how much I had been affected by sharing a room with Preston. Like the children, I have a strong sense of space, of needing a place that belongs just to me where I can go to be alone. Even when I was married, we always managed a study that belonged to me, where I could withdraw from the swirl of others' lives and be by myself. Maybe all people feel this way, I don't know. But my two children and I need this kind of private space.

"You really have no grounds," my lawyer told me in the spring. "But we do have a precedent. Your son has been living with you for almost two years, even though his mother has custody. Legal custody, I mean. Will the children tell the judge what I tell them to say?"

"About what?"

"Their mother. Why they want to live with you."

"I doubt it . . . I mean, if you want them to vilify their mother, no. They love their mother. They just prefer to live with me."

I realized I wasn't being very helpful, but I wasn't going to instruct the children to say things about their mother they didn't feel. Or that weren't true.

"Do you want custody of your daughter?" he asked. "Do you understand how flimsy our case is?"

"It is essential that she move in. She already has, emotionally. I've taken her to a psychiatrist who knows the family and he thinks it's imperative that she move in. He's willing to testify."

"Okay. Listen, you've got to do exactly what I tell you to do. You've got to stand on that window ledge stark naked and flap your arms in the air if I tell you to. You've got to do whatever I tell you to do, regardless of what you think. This isn't a gentleman's-club affair. If you want to win, you've got to do what I tell you. Is that agreed?"

I felt slightly sick to my stomach. Although it was vital that Molly move in, I couldn't be a part of something like this. Yet I knew I had to.

In the taxi on the way back to my office I unexpectedly remembered Molly's return from the hospital as a tiny infant. What a different scene. I wasn't standing naked on a window ledge, flapping my arms at the instructions of a lawyer. I was an extremely proud father and husband. The day she was to leave the hospital, I went to the baby boutique at Saks. I don't know if it still exists, I haven't been a new father in a number of years. Then it was filled with delightful little lace-trimmed silk dresses and lace-trimmed bonnets. I arrived at the hospital with my purchases and handed them to the nurse who was preparing my daughter for her first foray into the world. Mother and daughter left Doctors Hospital in style.

"I haven't seen one of these in years," our German nannie said when she was presented with her charge.

"What?" I asked.

"A bonnet. Save it. She'll like it when she grows up."

I have no idea where the bonnet is, or the long lovely silk dress I bought. Totally impractical, never to be used again. But I was not only the father of a fantastic son, I now had a beautiful daughter and I loved my wife and the world was possible.

Molly couldn't have been more than two weeks old when we, Molly's mother, Nannie and I, were sitting in the study watching television. Vanessa was wearing a flowing dressing gown—a welcome-home-from-the-hospital gift from a very happy father—and Nannie was mending some of Preston's handed-down baby clothes, when President Kennedy pre-empted normal programming to inform us we were on the verge of war with Russia over the Cuban missile situation. I sat spellbound. There was a twenty-six-month-old son sleeping in the nursery, a two-week-old daughter in a portable crib in the living room, where she was living with Nannie, a beautiful wife still recovering from a difficult delivery, and the world was falling apart. The first thing that crossed my mind was: Why had I been a part of bringing two more victims of such unreasoned hatred into the world?

After the President's speech we were all silent for a long time. "She doesn't have any eyelashes," I said, breaking the heavy silence.

"They will grow," said Nannie, who had seen numerous little girls through the same period of development. "They will grow."

"Preston had eyelashes that looked pasted on . . . those thick mink things models wear . . . when I saw him an hour after he was born. It really isn't fair for the boy of the family to have good eyes. Girls should have good eyelashes, not boys. And boys should not have to fight goddamn wars."

The festive, domestic air had evaporated. Nannie continued to mend, Vanessa lit a cigarette and we sat silently for a long time. What a shitty world my children were inheriting. I had no real inkling it could get even worse, that there would be the agony of Vietnam, Nixon, all the rest.

Nannie had been right. Molly grew the same kind of eyelashes Preston had. And as I sat in the taxi on the way back to my office, I wondered how I was going to feel when I stood naked on the window ledge, waving my arms, in order to gain custody of what had once been a fragile little thing in a silk bonnet with lace around the front.

"Possession is the way we go," my lawyer informed me a few days later. "What are your summer plans?"

"I have to attend a conference in Miami at the end of June. I had thought of taking the children along."

"That's how we work it. You pick up your daughter the day before you are to leave for Miami. Make it a routine thing. I'll make our announcement after you leave. You'll have physical custody. The mother will have to make the first move. We'll wait for her reaction and then see what we can do."

The Molly of the silk bonnet was now almost fourteen. Her parents, both of whom loved her, were engaged in a messy, never-to-be-forgotten, or -forgiven, war for her physical presence. After the Miami conference I took the children to Nassau to prolong the return to New York as long as possible. Paradise Island was quiet, the hotel half filled, the food and service almost adequate. We sat on the beach, read, snorkled, pretending all was well. I must say, both children are very calm in situations such as this. Neither of them show any signs of agitation or trepidation when we seem on the brink of a messy problem. Not Preston in Yugoslavia, nor Molly in Nassau. I don't know whether or not it is because they assume all will be well, or that, somehow, I will take care of things; regardless, there was no moment of tension while we were away. I had deliberately given no one our address in Nassau. I wanted to be surprised, not warned.

I can never know what went through Vanessa's mind during those terrible days when she knew her daughter, as well as her son, had elected to live with their father. But the qualities that attracted me to her in the first place, the reason I married her, had risen to the top; the sense of acceptance of what is, the sense of moving on, of not using the children as an avenue of revenge, made me respect her. It takes a great deal of personal courage for a woman, a mother, to become the other side of a routine divorce arrangement; to have the children visit her on alternate weekends, alternate holidays. Out of her love for Molly, she did not take us to court.

When I realized there was no necessity for me to stand on my lawyer's window ledge and flap my arms, I felt like mush inside. Now I was responsible for the emotional and physical well-being of both my children. The elation was tempered with a healthy amount of doubt . . . but I knew I had to make it work.

XIII

Since I already knew, or at least suspected, what my colleagues' reaction to Molly's move would be, it was pointless to bring it up until she actually lived with me. The whole subject of custody was no longer something my friends discussed with me. I was unpleasantly surprised to learn I had grossly underestimated the depth of their disapprobation. When I mentioned to a woman associate that my daughter was living with me, she nearly exploded.

"You mean you've really taken a young girl away from her mother? Are you out of your mind? You can't raise a girl."

"My son is doing fine."

"But that's entirely different. A father and son is one thing. You can tell each other dirty stories and drink beer together. A girl needs a woman to relate to."

"Molly needed a brother to relate to. Isn't it possible that boys need to relate to males every bit as much as girls need to have women around? No one mentioned that it was wrong for me to leave Preston with his mother when we separated. There appears to be some very confused thinking going on."

My associate poked furiously at the ice in her glass with a plastic stick. Obviously she didn't agree with me and I knew I had little chance of convincing her. More and more women I've talked to recently have undisguised hostility toward men—not just their ex-husbands, but men in general. I often feel awkward when I rush to open a door only to have my companion stalk through as though I had insulted her. Growing up in the South certainly has its drawbacks in the liberated world of New York. As graciously as possible I shifted the conversation to a project both of us were interested in, to neutral ground where my opinions and hers did not clash. We managed to get through the lunch as though nothing had happened. But as I was settling the check, she leaned over and put her hand on my arm, her gold bracelets clanking against my coffee cup. "You've made a terrible mistake, you know. I feel very sorry for your daughter."

What could I say? I smiled as brightly as I could and pulled her chair back as she rose to leave. I haven't called her since. We've exchanged notes on business matters a few times, but there seems little reason to go through that again. Unfortunately her opinion was the rule, not the exception.

The only positive comment I heard from a woman was, oddly enough, also a very negative one. "How lucky for you. She'll be able to help you around the house. Help cook and clean."

Freely translated, Molly could become the cook and maid for her father and brother. It smacked of a scene from an O'Neill play. One of the first things I had insisted on when Molly came in was that all household chores be shared equally. Molly wasn't to do the "feminine" chores, Preston the "masculine." Alternate nights to do the dishes, both help with the laundry, the picking up. Preston goes to the supermarket with me in order to lug the cart up and down curbs and steps; Molly unpacks and puts away. Since she enjoys cooking, once a week or so, she experiments in the kitchen, but cooking is basically my job. Often she bakes cookies or a cake after school, but she does so because she wants to, not because it's a female's job to do the baking. Occasionally, on weekends, Preston also bakes cookies. Although we now have a cleaning woman who does the ironing, both children can and often do iron their own clothes. Preston thinks no more about ironing a shirt than Molly thinks about taking out the garbage. Why should they?

In the beginning Molly was embarrassed to go shopping with me for her clothes, especially if she needed such things as new bras or panties. Rather than put her through it, I asked a friend to take her to a store when she needed something she thought too personal to deal with in the presence of a male, even her father. "Why do you talk about bras?" she wanted to know. "Mom never discussed Preston's jockstraps." Another area where my presence makes her uncomfortable is in the beauty parlor. Again, I find a woman to fill in.

I have long been aware that women at parties seem inclined to bunch together, excluding men from their conversations. This "girl talk" syndrome appears to develop very early. Molly had been living with me only a few weeks when she asked if she could invite some of her new friends from school for a "boy-girl" party. Teen-age parties, according to the stories I've heard, can be frightening affairs for parents, but I was delighted she had made friends so quickly and agreed to the idea. "Please stay out of the party," Molly begged.

"What would you like me to do? I'm not going out for the evening and leave you here alone with your friends. I'll work in my bedroom. Is that all right?"

"I guess so, but stay out of the living room, okay?"

Preston and I felt like prisoners in our rooms. I could hear the record player and occasional giggles, but there seemed to be very little activity going on. After nearly two hours I ventured through the living room to the kitchen—and found all the girls huddled in Molly's room, the boys sprawled on the floor in the living room, not even talking to one another. What kind of a party was this? I had feared wild dancing, heavy necking, drugs. Various mothers arrived to claim their children around eleven. It was a most tame affair.

"Why were the girls in your room, the boys in the living room?" I asked Molly when we were alone.

"The girls don't like the boys very much."

"Then why did you ask them?"

"You can't have a boy-girl party without boys."

Molly had the same difficulty at school establishing the fact that she lived with her father as Preston had had. The reaction of her friends whose parents were divorced was also much the same as Preston's. None of the girls wanted to live with their fathers and considered Molly a bit wacky for having moved in with me. There were the predictable embarrassed silences on the other end of the line when parent volunteers called to talk to Molly's mother, only to learn she was living with her father.

It would be misleading to imply there were no frictions,

no evenings when I wondered how I was going to handle the next day and the day after that. In the beginning Molly found it difficult to share the give-and-take of the life Preston and I had established before she moved in. Unfortunately, I had moved a television set into her room and soon she was spending the entire evening before the tube, coming out only to fix herself a glass of ginger ale. One evening she informed me she was going to take her dinner to her room so she could watch a program. When I insisted that she remain at the table she broke into tears and refused to eat, sitting there like a tear-stained Buddha. When I finally excused her she rushed into her room and slammed the door so hard that the mirror on the back nearly shattered.

In a number of magazine articles I've read recently, I've learned women are just beginning not to feel guilty because they become angry with their children. I felt no guilt whatsoever when I threw Molly's door open and demanded an apology. She was weeping uncontrollably on her bed. "Please leave me alone. I've got to work this out by myself. Please go away."

"Not before you apologize for being unnecessarily rude. You simply will not get by with such behavior here. You must understand that. I love you very much, but I cannot allow behavior like tonight's little scene. Do you want to discuss what's really bothering you?"

Through her sobs she apologized and I left her alone. Within fifteen minutes she returned to the living room. Preston was in his room doing homework. And it all poured out. Why she had been spending so much time alone in her room, her particular wish to be alone this night. The crowd of girls she had first gotten to know at school, the ones who had come to her party, had decided for reasons only another teen-ager would understand, not to have anything more to do with her. Molly, unlike Preston, needs friends and she had been cut off and didn't know why or which way to turn. And there was something else bothering her which she didn't bring up directly, but I felt it lurking around the edges of our conversation. For two years Preston and I had lived in the city without her; our routines were established. She was miserable at school and felt like an outsider in her own home.

Molly was obviously hurt and upset about the treatment she had received from her fair-weather school friends. Unfortunately, part of growing up is learning not to count too heavily on long-lasting friendships. She would have to deal with that herself. What I had to deal with was her relationship with her brother and me. She simply could not spend so much time alone, withdrawing from the life around her. I also knew, because of Preston's experience, that she felt guilty because she had hurt her mother by deciding to live with me. But the deed was done and a heavy load of guilt is difficult for a sensitive young girl to carry.

For the next few weeks I often joined her in her room and watched television with her, or we would talk. And without my having to say anything to Preston, he started joining us in Molly's room during his breaks between assignments. I began suggesting that the three of us return to the living room, where there was more space. It was a slow process, but it worked. Molly became a part of things, no longer hiding away in her room like a wounded animal. She made new friends at school, and she and Preston began going out to the movies without me. She was getting her sea legs.

It became very important to me that the children consider our apartment a home in the real sense of what a home should be. Single men I know never consider the place they live in a "home." A bachelor apartment is a way station, a place to stash your gear between other involvements. It wasn't until Molly moved in that I fully realized how important it is for me to have a place where I feel settled. To be a home, an apartment must have a sense of permanence, an atmosphere of shared interests; a place which reflects, through the choice of art on the walls, the style of furniture, the individual personality of the people living there.

The apartment I now share with my children is actually the first home I have had that I truly consider my own. While growing up, I obviously shared my parents' home, but that reflected their tastes, not mine. During World War II, four years of college, the Korean War, I had a place to sleep, but I was always in transit, never mentally unpacking and settling down. When I was married, the apartments we rented and the house we eventually bought were really Vanessa's. It was she who decided on the color of the carpet, where the furniture would be placed, what kind of a refrigerator we should have. I was allowed to pick out "my" chair for the living room, or decide on which wall to put the bookshelves in the study, but the apartments, the house, were essentially feminine in tone; as they should, I might add. I wasn't prevented from putting my imprint on our life style; I merely considered it Vanessa's right to live the way she wanted to. That's the old cultural myth that the inside of the house belongs to the wife, and the basement, the garage and the yard to the husband. Even the apartment I shared with Preston for a year and a half wasn't really a home; there was always a sense of "camping out" with both of us sharing the bedroom. I had known we would be moving as soon as I could afford to.

I have involved the children in every purchase of furniture, blinds, paintings, carpets, because I want them to feel toward the apartment as I do; that it represent for them a real home with the sense of security and warmth only a permanent home can provide.

We are also accumulating an "extended family." Marion and Tony Basta live two floors below us. They have no children and are among the few people we know who are not either embarrassed or somehow intimidated by the fact the children are living with their father. Marion is available when Molly needs to share secrets only a female will understand. Tony and Preston have established a relationship independent from the group. The Bastas are like the people who live in the house next door in small towns across the country. We have keys to their apartment and collect their mail and water their plants when they are away, as they do for us. The five of us often go out to dinner together, stop by each other's apartment for drinks, share our successes and failures. Mario and Adrian Viscovich, a young couple from Yugoslavia we met after our vacation there, have become the people on the next block. We don't see them as regularly as the Bastas, but they too accept our living arrangements without feeling sorry for the children. Adrian is a teacher and has helped Molly feel more secure academically.

Talking of friends in New York City in terms of small-town relationships may seem odd—but it isn't odd for me. After Molly had been in the city for a year, our life settled down to a routine not unlike life in many small towns

—with obvious differences, of course. We're living in the heart of Manhattan, but we shop in the same stores, use the same dry cleaners week after week. They all know us, we know them.

There are also great contrasts from the small-town life I once knew. The conversations at dinner are certainly different from what I remember. We often discuss South Africa, North Ireland, Cambodia, Greek-Turkish conflicts. My children are aware of the world, they are concerned about things I knew nothing about at their age. But still we have managed to build for ourselves a small haven in the swirling life of New York. It is as though my life has gone full cycle; I am now looking for the simpler existence I once knew, rediscovering the satisfying joys of sharing my children's lives my parents must have known.

I suppose I am trying to give my children the best of two worlds—the one I knew and the one I discovered when I began wandering the globe in search of my private grail. I want them to feel secure enough in the life we live so that they have the courage to explore and find the kind of life which best fits their own interests and needs when it is time for them to move on.

One evening when Molly and I were alone she asked me if I was ever going to get married again. "Preston will be leaving next year for college. In three years, I'll be going away to college and you'll be alone."

"Do you want a stepmother?"

"Good heavens, no. I was just thinking about your being left alone."

"I can manage, I really can. Anyway, I haven't met anyone I would want to live with. Maybe, if I do, I'll marry again. But don't worry about me; I'll be fine."

During the time before Preston moved in, I had given some thought to establishing a long-lasting relationship, but both children were openly hostile toward anyone I introduced them to if they suspected something permanent in the wind. Their reaction was quite normal; they saw so little of me that they were jealous of anyone who shared their time with me. The urgent need to plunge into another relationship slowly faded. My children were more important to me than having an affair.

I'm no good in the one-night stand situation; I've never been and hope I never will think that life style satisfying. I've settled for a monklike existence as long as the children are around. It isn't that I don't sometimes wake up in the morning and wish there were someone I loved in bed beside me. But I'm not in love and I can't accept anything less; I'm simply not that desperate.

"All my friends' fathers have girl friends and their mothers have boyfriends," Molly informed me.

"I hope they are happy. I'm content the way things are."

Molly's plans for the future include being an actress. I can't fault her for that; I came up to New York originally to study acting and quickly found I wasn't cut out for a theatrical career. I love going to the theater, but I often have work to do in the evenings and the children have homework, so we don't see many plays, certainly not as many as Molly wants to see. I suggested she take a friend to a Wednesday afternoon performance—her school is only half-day on Wednesdays. The first time she went with a friend, it didn't turn out too well. Her friend wanted to have lunch at one place, Molly another (the choice, I should point out, was between two fast-food shops). So, two weeks later, Molly announced she was going downtown alone. I was nervous, it seemed a daring thing to do at her age, but I didn't want to be overprotective, so I agreed. Since then she has seen virtually every musical and play currently running on Broadway—by herself. Many of her friends' mothers think I'm taking a terrible risk, allowing her to go to the theater alone. How else is she going to learn to feel independent, to feel free enough to do the things in life she wants to do? As I write this, Molly is living in a state of suspended animation. Her French teacher is taking a small group of students from school to France for spring vacation—an educational tour of the Loire Valley and Paris. For Molly, this is a repeat. What is new is that for the first time, she will be traveling without her father. One of the things both children have learned from me is to never allow their passports to expire.

Preston is also in a state of suspended animation, trying not to think about April when college acceptances—or rejections—start coming in. He decided a number of years ago he wanted to go into medical research—not be a doctor who has to deal with patients, but a man who seeks answers to medical problems. It is sometimes painful to think it has all gone so fast. I have encouraged him to apply to colleges outside New York, but close enough to economically afford to come in for weekends if he wants to. I will certainly miss him, and quite selfishly hope he will sometimes miss the life we have had together, but not too often. We can remain friends only if he knows he is his own man, that he doesn't have to fight against me to establish his own life.

Sometimes I feel my life is a long downhill ride, picking up speed as the days and weeks and months rush by. But I have no regrets. I am making the most of each day as it flits past, grabbing moments here and there that will linger long after the children have lives of their own.

Because time goes by so fast, I find it difficult to understand men of my generation who have missed the experiences I have had—and hope to continue to have—with my children. I know for certain that most of them are much better off financially than I am, they are more important in their organizations, more successful in the American sense of being successful. I do not envy them their success, it would be pointless to feel sorry for them; they haven't an idea of what they've missed. If you don't like the taste of champagne, drink beer. Too many men I know are satisfied with warm beer.

XIV

It is much too late for my generation to change the direction of our lives; we're creatures of habit, accepting the sameness of our routines without the desire or the energy to alter the course of our existence. What's past is past; deal only with today and tomorrow.

The generation following us, young men in their late twenties and early thirties, appear unwilling to accept the world they have inherited. Taking their lead from the social unrest of the sixties and the thrust of the women's liberation movement, they are demanding rights as fathers that would never have occurred to us. I became aware of their concerns after the New York *Times* printed a short essay of mine accusing my generation of not really wanting their children because child care was, at the very least, inconvenient. The response was immediate. I received calls from young men from as far away as Buffalo, Albany, Baltimore, San Francisco, Kansas City. The first question each of the callers wanted answered was how I gained custody of my children. I couldn't be very helpful. I had not faced a long and costly court battle. Fortunately for my children and me, the woman I married was unique, a person with the maturity to put the welfare of the children above her own ego needs.

The men who called were not so lucky. The stories they told me were heartbreaking. One young man told me his wife had fallen in love with another man and had abruptly left for California, taking his six-month-old-son with her. Was there any way he could get his son back? Another told me his wife had moved away while he was on a business trip, taking his two children and leaving no forwarding address. He had no idea where his children were. All the stories were similar. A single thread ran through one sad episode after another. These fathers were being denied their legal and moral rights to their children. The wives were still operating under the traditional theory that the mother, and only the mother, had any right to children. Unlike my generation which, while heartbroken, would have accepted their fate in sullen silence, the men who called me were determined to fight back, to establish if at all possible equal rights to their children.

"If I promise never to try to see my daughter again," one man told me, "she will never ask for a cent of alimony or support. Never see my daughter again! Can you believe that?"

"And if you don't promise?"

"If I don't promise, she will ruin me financially. Her father put money into my business when we were married. He told me it was a gift. But if I don't promise not to see my daughter again, she will insist on taking the money back. I'll be ruined. I'm just getting started."

"What is more important, your daughter or your business?"

He paused for a moment. I could hear him breathing into the phone. "In truth, my daughter. To hell with the business. I just want my daughter."

He was of the new generation. My career-oriented friends would have answered that question quite differently.

Unfortunately, there were no words of wisdom, no legal advice, I could pass on to those desperate young men. I'm not a lawyer or a judge or a member of a legislature. I am simply a man who slid into the caring for his children, at first reluctantly. I share their anguish, I went through it when I had to leave my children, but they are not taking their loss lying down the way I did. They are going to fight back and some of them are going to win.

The one thing which surprised me more than that the men were sufficiently concerned for their children to want to fight for them was that their wives were so determined to keep them. The reaction of the young and supposedly liberated wives was the same as their older, nonliberated sisters. Most of the wives of the men who have been in touch with me are career women, demanding equal rights in the marketplace. I find it difficult to believe these young women do not realize that in a reordered society they are helping to establish, they are going to have to equally share the lives of their children with their ex-husbands.

These young women are in for a surprise. The male finally is waking up. He is organizing, he is no longer willing to shrug his shoulders and walk away when his rights as a father are denied him. Both my children were living with me before I became aware of the movement spreading across the country. There are now more than eighty groups of divorced fathers who collectively are fighting to change the public's attitude toward divorce and child custody. They are refusing to be cast out of their children's lives like no-longer-needed old shoes; men who are pulling together to break the strangle hold the female has on children.

Up until two or three years ago, the wife was always considered the victim in any divorce action, regardless of why a marriage fell apart. The laws (written by male-dominated legislatures) were specifically designed to protect the future of the injured party—the wife. Progress is going to be slow, but cracks have already appeared in the protective wall around the wife/mother. A leading child psychologist recently won custody in New York of his two children because he was better able to provide the children with the cultural and emotional atmosphere they needed to develop into functioning adults. The difference between the doctor and less fortunate fathers is that he had the money to sustain a long and very costly court battle. A judge in Massachusetts recently awarded a father custody—and child support from his ex-wife—of his seven-year-old daughter. The New York State Court of Appeals ruled unanimously in 1977 that a woman must pay child support to her former husband who retained custody of their child when they were divorced four years earlier. Another victory for the male was a ruling in April 1977 by the Mississippi Supreme Court, which ruled that a divorced woman was not automatically entitled to receive alimony if she was able to find a job. At least some progress is being made.

Very little research has been done on the effects of a divorce on the male. Somehow, we are supposed to just fade away when we are kicked out of the house we once shared with our children; we are not to interfere with the day-to-day lives of our sons and daughters. Just send the check on time and don't be resentful when that check contributes to the support of the ex-wife's boyfriend.

Before my generation began trooping to the divorce courts by the millions, divorce was not a generally acceptable solution to a family's problem. Whether staying together and suffering through a lifetime of unhappiness was the right solution or not is today quite academic. There have been endless studies which conclude that an unhappy marriage is just as damaging to children as a divorce. But if divorce is to be a workable solution, then the whole process has to be rethought. There can no longer be the assumption that the mother will automatically have custody of the children. A father must have the same rights before the courts as the mother. And the rights of children must be guaranteed, not assumed.

There is a strange irony in the struggle just getting under way. It is really a struggle between youth and age, between fresh ideas and clichés. It is not a struggle between men and women, but between men and men. It is the male who must be re-educated to understand that the ability to nurture children is learned, not inherited.

Margaret Mead has written that humans are "dependent neither on instinct nor on genetically transmitted specific capabilities but on learned ways of life that accumulated slowly through endless borrowing, readaptation, and innovation."

Ashley Montagu has noted that as a race, we do not rely on instincts for our survival.

> It is not that nothing at all has been left of our biological heritage, but that humans have evolved under the pressure of problem-solving challenges from the cultural and physical environments. As a consequence, humans have moved into a new zone of adaptation in which their behavior is dominated by learned responses, *not* by predetermined reactions. It is within the dimension of culture, the learned, the human-made part of the environment, that humans grow, develop, and function as behaving organisms. And it is the cultural environment that has exerted the greatest pressure in molding humans not only culturally but also physically.

The nurturing of the young is something humans learn, not inherit. Since girls are taught from early youth that their role is to "mother," they grow to maturity with a "learned" reaction to their offspring. The young boy is taught just the opposite. Even today, I notice mothers of young boys warning them not to cry if they are hurt or sad or disappointed. To feel emotions is "feminine," even in today's liberated age.

My generation is dominated by emotionally crippled men unable to comprehend that younger men have not only the desire but the ability to care for their children. They sit looking down from the bench at young men pleading for an equal chance to participate in their children's lives without the foggiest idea of what the young men are asking for. Who knows what goes on in the minds of judges? There certainly is a mixture of outworn clichés about mothering, the role of a father as merely the provider, all the other cultural stigmas against the male who is capable of feeling and sharing emotions.

Quite frankly, I don't believe that the majority of young men today really want the burden of taking care of children. Nor do I believe that all of those who do want custody are really prepared to adequately provide what their children need. But the growing number who do want and can care for children should not be victims of a system that automatically excludes them from gaining custody unless they can prove that their ex-wives are depraved or mentally incompetent. From conversations with men my age, I found that most of them believe custody battles are really nothing more than a chance to get back at the ex-wife, an act of revenge rather than a plea for a chance to share in the lives of their children. Since they never wanted to care for their own, they assume there is only a motive of revenge behind any custody battle. How little they know—and how much they have missed!

In this battle of male against male for custody, the children are the real losers. When are we as a society going to begin to truly consider the rights and needs of children? How many more children are going to be turned out into the world emotionally wounded, bitter, incapable of loving and being loved because their parents used them as pawns and judges ignored their rights?

My generation is in what Erik Erikson calls the seventh stage of life. The six stages before were developmental, the slow process of finding one's identity. The seventh stage is one in which we are established in our careers, where we are at our most productive; it is an age of responsibility, of living life to the fullest, a time to be creative, to produce. It is also the age of generativity, of parenting and caring for the next generation. Not to care, according to Erikson, is stagnation, a slipping into the eighth stage, where the juices of life begin to dry up, to become bitter, lonely souls without a reason or purpose or meaning for our existence.

The young men who have awakened to their own need to be real fathers, who understand that life is complete only when one has accepted the sense of generation, have a difficult path ahead of them. When women began demanding equal rights, they were essentially fighting only on one front—against the male-oriented society. Young fathers must fight a two-front battle—one against females who refuse to admit the male has any rights to their children, and one against the established male-dominated judicial system, which acts as the legal instrument for the female point of view. Many will lose their children for every one who succeeds. As women have learned, the only way to win is to band together, to become a large enough and powerful enough force to command the attention of the courts and legislatures. Individual tilts at the windmill will surely be futile. Our society is too encrusted with the barnacles of cultural myths to change without a major revolution to wipe out the outworn values held so dear by those in power.

I have been fortunate; a number of those barnacles have been scraped from my life. I didn't, however, do the scraping; Preston and Molly did. The two of them have taught me something I never knew, nor really suspected before—that to love and respect your children and to be loved by them is all one can ultimately hope for in the space of time we can know. Traditionally, the young are to learn from their elders. The young can also teach us a great deal if we take the time to listen, not just with our heads, but listen with our whole being. I owe my children more than they will ever know. I hope the young fathers who truly want their children and are willing to fight for them have the opportunity to experience the life I share with my children. Such a life is well worth the battle.

About the Author

LINLEY M. STAFFORD grew up in Kentucky but has considered New York home base since the end of World War II. He was an executive in broadcasting and is now manager of New York public relations for the National Education Association. He lives in New York with his two children.